Precision Archery

Precision Archery

Steve Ruis
Claudia Stevenson
Editors

Human Kinetics

Library of Congress Cataloging-in-Publication Data

Precision archery / edited by Steve Ruis and Claudia Stevenson.
    p. cm.
Includes bibliographical references and index.
    ISBN 0-7360-4634-8 (softcover)
    1. Archery. I. Ruis, Steve, 1946- II. Stevenson, Claudia, 1954-
    GV1185.P74 2004
    799.3'2--dc21

                               2003014776
ISBN: 0-7360-4634-8

The Web addresses cited in this text were current as of August 2003, unless otherwise noted.

Acquisitions Editor: Ed McNeely; **Developmental Editor:** Laura Pulliam; **Assistant Editor:** Alisha Jeddeloh; **Copyeditor:** Patsy Fortney; **Proofreader:** Jennifer L. Davis; **Indexers:** Robert and Cynthia Swanson; **Graphic Designer:** Nancy Rasmus; **Permission Manager:** Toni Harte: **Graphic Artist:** Francine Hamerski; **Art & Photo Manager:** Dan Wendt; **Cover Designer:** Keith Blomberg; **Photographers (cover and interior):** Steve Ruis and Claudia Stevenson unless otherwise noted; **Illustrator:** Steve Ruis; **Printer:** United Graphics

Human Kinetics books are available at special discounts for bulk purchase. Special editions or book excerpts can also be created to specification. For details, contact the Special Sales Manager at Human Kinetics.

Printed in the United States of America 10 9 8 7 6 5 4 3 2 1

Human Kinetics
Web site: www.HumanKinetics.com

United States: Human Kinetics
P.O. Box 5076
Champaign, IL 61825-5076
800-747-4457
e-mail: humank@hkusa.com

Canada: Human Kinetics
475 Devonshire Road Unit 100
Windsor, ON N8Y 2L5
800-465-7301 (in Canada only)
e-mail: orders@hkcanada.com

Europe: Human Kinetics
107 Bradford Road
Stanningley
Leeds LS28 6AT, United Kingdom
+44 (0) 113 255 5665
e-mail: hk@hkeurope.com

Australia: Human Kinetics
57A Price Avenue
Lower Mitcham, South Australia 5062
08 8277 1555
e-mail: liaw@hkaustralia.com

New Zealand: Human Kinetics New Zealand
Division of Sports Distributors NZ Ltd.
P.O. Box 300 226 Albany
North Shore City, Auckland
0064 9 448 1207
e-mail: blairc@hknewz.com

This book is dedicated to all of the archery coaches—past, present, and future—who have helped us along the way and who will be helping the millions of new archers to come.

Contents

Preface

Have you ever made a perfect shot? I remember one in particular. Claudia and I were in an archery training camp at the Olympic Training Center in Chula Vista, California. I was shooting at 70m. I made such a good shot that I said, "That's a ten," before it was called through a spotting scope. "That's a ten," came the reply from the spotter. I love that feeling! Shortly thereafter, I had another such shot. Again I called my shot, "That's a ten." "That's a six," came the call from the spotter. I was dead right of the ten ring. What went wrong? It was simply that I hadn't yet learned to read the little flags atop the target that tell you about the wind.

There is a lot to learn to become an excellent archer. Really good archers differ from good archers in that they have slightly more "perfect shots." A perfectly executed shot that doesn't take a significant wind into account is not a perfect shot. So, getting all the knowledge you can about archery is a good thing, yes? Well, yes and no. The danger of filling your head with everything you can learn is that every bit of archery knowledge you acquire can also get in your way and prevent you from making those shots. So, the challenge is to learn all you can, then ingrain that knowledge into your shot, then shoot for the sheer unadulterated joy of shooting. The secret is, when you get advice, make sure you get good advice—that's why we have enlisted *Archery Focus* magazine's best teachers, coaches, and champions to provide you with a pathway to excellence in archery. Enjoy!

—Steve Ruis
Editor, *Archery Focus* magazine

Why archery? I often have to laugh at myself and my relationship to archery. The way I struggle with my form, my equipment, and my mental game makes me wonder why I bother. The way I turn to archery for relaxation, focus, community, and fun makes me wonder what I would do without it. For me, archery serves as a metaphor for my life. The joys and frustrations, the routine and discipline (or lack thereof), the contact with other archers who are aiming for the same goal but approaching it very differently—all of these things show me who I am. It is no mystery to me why archery has been used for centuries as a tool for meditation and spiritual development. But it is "just archery," which means I can have it any way I want. I want to have fun. I want to compete. I want to offer this book (in addition to *Archery Focus* magazine) to you, kindred archer. May this ancient, high-tech, demanding, fascinating sport enrich your life as it has mine. See you at the range.

—Claudia Stevenson
Managing Editor, *Archery Focus* magazine

Introduction

Welcome to *Archery Focus* magazine's *Precision Archery!* If you are just beginning in archery we recommend you start with *Archery: Steps to Success* by Haywood and Lewis (Human Kinetics 1997). If you have been an archer for a while but feel that you could be shooting much better than you are—this book is for you. If you have been away from archery and are coming back to it—this book is for you. If you want to compete—and win—this book is for you! Here, all in one place, you will find much of the information you need to excel at archery. Master archers and coaches will lead you through all the mazes surrounding archery equipment, physical and mental skills, tuning, practice, and competition.

Rick McKinney, many-time world and Olympic champion, will guide you through the ins and outs of competition. Renowned coaches Don Rabska and Larry Wise will show you what a champion's form looks like. Archery Focus magazine's fitness and mental skill gurus, Annette M. Musta and Dr. Lisa Franseen, will show you how to train your body and mind to function at a championship level. You will learn how to tune your recurve and compound bows to minimize the errors you make in shooting. We'll even help you find and work with a coach, learn to shoot in the wind and rain, how to practice for maximum progress, and how to work through the inevitable difficulties that come up. All of these authors have years of experience as archers, coaches, and writers. They have written articles and whole books on archery and now bring together their collected wisdom to help you reach your archery goals.

Each chapter can be read alone or as part of the whole course of topics. You are going to want to put things into practice right away, so don't hesitate to put the book aside and grab your bow. Just reading this book won't make you a better archer if you don't put what you read into practice.

All chapters contain photos, diagrams, and exercises to illustrate and drive home the points the authors are making. Much of the material applies to all archers, while some is specific to those of you shooting recurve bows, and some is specific to those of you who shoot compound bows. We urge you to read the whole book, though, as it is often the case that things you read that are seemingly far afield can help you the understand the problems you are working on.

The first chapter starts you right out in the crucible of excellence, competition. Whether you just want to improve yourself or you just want to win, Rick McKinney tells you why competition provides the arena for improvement. The preparation, the pressure, the drive to score—all stress the ability to perform. If you want to compete at a high level and win, you need a plan. Rick will help you prepare one. Next Don Rabska (for recurve archers) and Larry Wise (for compound archers) discuss the ins and outs of form, the foundation of the shot. You've probably heard the claim, "You don't have to do it right; you just have to do it the same way every time," or "The recipe for high level archery has only two steps: 1. Shoot a perfect shot, and 2. Repeat." It is having form that works with your physical makeup that makes the repetition necessary for high scores possible. Once you have a physical foundation for a repeatable shot, we will address how to execute each shot to maximize your success.

You may not need any more than what the first four chapters offer, but there is a wealth of additional material—Annette M. Musta on strength, conditioning, and flexibility programs and guidance; Dr. Lisa Franseen provides an introduction to mental skills programs and their value with specific suggestions; Rick Stonebraker (for recurve archers) and Steve Ruis and Claudia Stevenson (for compound archers) treat advanced bow fitting (draw weight, draw length, stabilization), bow tuning (brace height, plunger adjustments, etc.), arrow tuning (archer's paradox, vanes/feathers, spine, point mass, FOC, etc.); M.J. Rogers on everything from how to find a coach to working with him/her, to leaving him/her; and Steve Ruis and Claudia Stevenson teach you how to deal with difficulties ranging from dealing with wind and rain while shooting, to target/clicker panic, then cover how to test new equipment. Some archers try to buy a better score. This can even work. For example, by replacing a set of often bent and often straightened aluminum arrows with a new set, your shot will improve. But how much improvement is there? Will better equipment automatically make you a better archer? What about the Hawthorne Effect *(Everything new seems good—at first)*? Steve and Claudia will show you how you can determine whether a new gizmo is worth it. They finish with a chapter on perfecting your practice sessions.

You can start anywhere in this book, but if your goal is excellence you will find it necessary to cover it all. Good shooting.

Exploring Competition

Have you ever dreamed of being a member of a national team and competing for your country? It is a rare youngster who hasn't had such dreams. In 1981 the United States Archery Team (USAT) of the National Archery Association (NAA) was formed. It was created as a fund-raising tool for the NAA and to train future world and Olympic champions. I was honored to be the volunteer to set up the training program. It also taught me a great deal about competition and competitors.

The one-week training camp was designed to bring together the top 10 male and female archers who were training for the Olympics. Twenty of the best archers in the United States would converge to share their knowledge, improve their skills, and offer insights into what it takes to reach such a high level. Coaches, scientists, and other professionals were also brought in to work with the archers.

The training camp had two goals: to help the archers improve their performances and to gather as much information as possible from the top archers so that this knowledge could be passed on to aspiring young archers and coaches. Although the program was an unqualified success for fund-raising and raised the bar of the overall performance of

Rick McKinney

the archers, a gap seemed to exist between being very good and being excellent. The United States Olympic Committee (USOC) considered the USAT program a model for other sports to follow, an accolade that gave the NAA prestige and funding, but still the level of excellence was not where it should have been. Many archers complained that they were not getting the level of information they wanted and that the time spent at the testing facilities constituted nothing more than time taken away from real training.

Not only did I leave frustrated, but I also wondered whether anyone would ever knock Darrell Pace and me out of the winner's circle. We had dominated the international scene since 1975 and were long overdue to be surpassed by better archers. The U.S. men's life expectancy in international events was about three years at the most. Darrell and I had dominated for twice that and were still going strong. This was nonetheless a sign of the decay of the U.S. dominance in international competition, and we needed someone to pick up the torch.

A few years later, in 1985, I had just won my third world title, and the USAT program was still receiving support from the USOC. Scientists were receiving awards for their research programs with the USAT and their testing and findings. The year before, Darrell Pace had won his second individual gold medal at the 1984 Olympics. Although the USAT program was still considered one of the best training camps, archers were not committed to it. Maybe this was because they were afraid of changing their habits. After all, who wants to take the chance of falling off the team while making a potentially unnecessary modification to one's form, equipment, or mental approach? No matter the reasons, there was no way to convince the elite archers to take a chance. Drastic measures had to be taken. Either we got these archers off their duffs, or we got to get them to quit and then, maybe, we could recruit archers who would be willing to try some of the new ideas being offered.

You see, nobody was trying any of the suggestions that were given at the camps! At the fall training camp, I decided to confront the participants and challenge them. I told them that none of them would ever beat me! This kind of statement was entirely out of character for me, and although I did not like being the bad guy, I had to try. They not only were stunned by my comments, but some stewed at the implications. My challenge implied that they did not have what it took, and were unwilling to make the effort, to become champions. It also told them that I was not giving out all of this information for fear of being beat but because I knew they would not listen or try any of the suggestions being offered. I told them they had been given every opportunity to improve themselves and not one had taken any of the advice given. I knew they would not improve or even be competitive because they were not willing to get out of their comfort zones and take that next step to improve their performance.

One archer took my challenge to heart. He considered what I said and agreed that, although there was a lot of good information given, he had not tried any of it. He decided to try some of the new ideas, and in 1988 he won the individual gold medal at the Seoul, Korea, Olympics. He attributes a major part of winning the gold to making the decision to take to heart the suggestions given at the USAT camps. Although Jay Barrs has commented about the USAT training camps and how the little speech given by an adversary sparked him, what he really did was just listen to all of the suggestions given, and then he tried most of them. He learned that all ideas are important to digest and test one way or another. He learned to filter what worked for him from what did not work for him, and he was able to develop a solid program and shape himself into a real champion.

I told you this story not because I think all of you will be in the Olympics, but because competition, at its core, involves taking chances and learning: learning about your sport, but more important, learning about yourself. To reach your goals, you need to absorb and digest ideas, taking from them the pieces that work for you. Being prepared to try new things when given the opportunity to excel is one of the most important attributes a competitor can have. It is essential if you want to be a champion.

Finding Your Level

Competing takes different shapes for different people. You may be competing against a friend in the backyard; against other "equals" in a club, state, regional, or even national event; or you may even be competing in the international, world, or Olympic arena. Each of these competitions has a purpose, and as an individual, you must figure out if you want to be a part of these specific arenas or if you prefer to shoot for the fun of it. Each of these events requires different capabilities for handling stress, and each of us has a stress level that we consider to be comfortable. It is important for you to find your level and learn how to get there fast. Learning more about yourself and what makes you tick will be of benefit as you progress up the stress level ladder from one event to another. Stress levels will change as your confidence changes because naturally it takes more capability to handle stress at a state-level competition than at a club-level competition. Your stress level may also depend on the degree of importance you place on the event. While some people consider a state-level competition very important, and therefore quite stressful, others may consider it to be of small meaning; thus they experience little, if any, stress at all.

Like many things in life, you need to learn to use the "baby step" method. Taking small steps to achieve one goal and then the next requires a lot of patience. Most of us want to go from zero to hero in a short amount of time and fail to see that it's not going to happen! Plus, you would lose the wonderful journey that you are about to take. I can assure you that the journey is far greater than the accomplishment. Enjoy the experience and learn from it and you will benefit far more than you will by gauging your success by trophy count alone. First, you must find the personal enjoyment of archery, and second, you must understand that once you have gathered experience, you acquire an edge that others who did not take time to learn do not have.

Joining the Competition

People choose to compete in archery for many reasons—to win, to test themselves, or just for the sheer fun of it. One of the stronger reasons is the social aspect of the sport. Many people like to spend time with their friends and meet new people, and there is probably no better place to find this than in archery. The social gatherings that occur in most clubs encourage people to get together and spend quality time with each other. Shooting together is a wonderful opportunity to cement relationships and have a good time. Not many people enjoy shooting alone.

The encouragement and challenge of fellow archers help us train, practice, and work at improving ourselves for the next event. This is why leagues are set up. This gets people out and setting up shooting schedules to work at improving their game. Another benefit is that you will learn more from discussing ideas with other archers than you will alone. Although not all ideas will work for any particular archer, it is important that you consider all of the possibilities to find those best suited for your physical form and personality. This takes time. Being with your friends is usually a better way to try out those different ideas.

© National Archery Association

Vic Wunderle, 2000 Olympic silver medalist, took a chance. He was a successful 3-D compound bow shooter, but switched to a recurve bow to pursue his Olympic dream.

On the other hand, some archers prefer to train and practice alone. They do not like to socialize during events, nor do they like chatting with others at practice. This isolation generates the extra stress they need to achieve a higher performance. One of the reasons "archery loners" may do well is that they feel alone during competition and are able to stay focused. These competitors enjoy the thrill of not knowing how others are scoring, only that they must stay internally focused to win or meet their goals. They tend to hope for the best but expect the worst. Although this appears to be a negative approach (some sport psychologists may argue differently), archers who are prepared for the worst but work at being the best usually do well. However, both ideas have to be understood for them to work hand in hand. There is no question that a confident person has a good chance of doing well, but a person who is both confident and prepared to take on all negative challenges will do well too. You will meet both of these kinds of competitors and more.

To Compete or Not to Compete

Some people are just plain competitive no matter what they do. You can tell who they are. They may try to beat you to a spot in the lunch line or to the door or some other little silly adventure that most people couldn't care less about. If you are this kind of person, there is very little need to encourage you to try competition. Your agenda is to avoid making foolish mistakes because of your need to win or beat someone. Learning to master your skills during a competition is a competition in itself. Learning how to compete with yourself will also give you an edge that most people do not take the time to learn.

Other people really don't like to compete. If you are one of these, you should recognize this and just enjoy shooting with your friends or enjoy mastering your game without fear of challenges from others. After all, people will judge you by how you compete, whether you like it or not. If your ego is rather large, competition will not work well for you unless you do well. If your ego is small and your self-esteem is good, then you should not have any problems with outside influences. If you are in the middle and enjoy competing and yet are not secure in your capabilities, do not feel alone! Many people fall within this category; this is another reason we compete.

If you are in the "in between" group, to master your insecurity you need to continue to test it. This requires you to participate in many tournaments—club, state, regional, or even national events. The more competitions you go to, the more you will master yourself and your sport.

Getting Zoned

If you do embrace competition, you will eventually find a "zone" where you are comfortable and compete at a high level. This zone is something that is very hard to achieve, yet it is the most sought-after place for a top archer. The zone is a feeling people get when they are able to achieve a higher-than-normal level of performance. Unfortunately, most of us cannot normally recall how we did it! When competing archers start shooting well during a competition, they just stay "in the groove" as long as they can. Although staying in the groove or the zone sounds easy, it is not. It takes as little as a wrong thought to have everything come crashing down. You can go from shooting your best to spiraling out of control and shooting poorly for no reason at all. Many people call this "choking," but I think that is a bit too harsh. It is more like losing a euphoric feeling and all at once being thrown back into mundane reality. The result is often total confusion. It literally throws you so off balance that you have a hard time getting back on track.

Getting *into* the zone is very challenging. Although most archers get into the zone at some point, it is extremely difficult to stay there for a long period of time. Most archers are good at it for maybe two arrows (which is why you may shoot two tens and then shoot poorly on the next shot). Essentially, you are finding a feeling or thought process that allows you to perform at your best. It requires a lot of discipline both physically and mentally to hold on to that mind-set and physicality. The physical part is easier to acquire, usually through extensive training on a blank bale and perfecting your form. The more your form becomes automatic (some say subconscious), the more consistent your form will be. This is the foundation for tremendous scoring capabilities. However, translating that form to actual winning scores requires a mental approach that allows your subconscious mind to take over the physical execution of each shot, thus providing for the consistency required to achieve high scores. This is the challenge for competing archers.

Staying focused on a simple procedure of executing shot after shot is normally too mundane for us, so our minds wander to the "glamorous" thoughts of winning, records, medals, fame, and so on. When this happens, you lose your zone and you are thrown out of the controlling safety of your subconscious mind. You become more conscious of your actions and lose the rhythm of your shooting. Your self-confidence breaks down, causing your form to break down even more. Then, at some point, you will calm down and realize that you need to focus on simple execution, and you then slip back into the zone without realizing it. Your scores climb until you get back into a wrong thought process and fall again.

Rarely can archers or any other kind of athlete stay in the zone during the course of an entire event. It does happen. It requires some luck, but mostly tremendous mental training. If excellent shooting is your goal, you need to develop the mental as well as the physical side of your archery. Many mental programs are available, some of which will be discussed in chapter 6. It is important that you have more than just one mental toolkit available. Sometimes your favorite mental approach just does not get you into the zone. This is when it is vitally important to have a backup, sort of like having a backup bow, string, tab, release, and so forth. You would never go into a major event without backup equipment; why would you go into this same event without a backup mental game plan?

A Word About Scoring

Dealing with scoring and scoring goals is one of the more difficult challenges you will experience. This is tied in with competition as we all know. Most of us set a score as our goal and are very familiar with where we are in a competition when it comes to score. But our score generates a tremendous amount of stress, which causes us to be distracted, confused, and often frustrated. Oh, I'm shooting a personal best! Oh, I am really shooting over my head! Oh, what a rotten score; I'll never reach my goal today! Sound familiar? That is why it is important to ignore your score, get into the zone, and stay there! Although score is highly important, it is also one of the most devastating parts of shooting.

For most people, the less they know about their scoring, the better off they are. Since score is a measure of how you are doing in comparison with everyone else, it can have a negative effect on both high- and low-scoring individuals. Archers would do well to focus on the actual execution of the shot or something of importance that will help the shot rather than the overall score. You may have heard of the Zen warrior's goal of "one shot, one life." This is the focus you need more than anything else. Only your final score has any meaning, and the only way to get a good final score is to execute one good shot and then repeat it. A "one shot at a time" approach helps you to get into the zone, and as long as you can stay focused on the present shot, you will stay in the zone.

Getting Prepped

How do you prepare for competition? Practice is important. Imagination is important. Determination is important. And . . . attitude is important. Most top archers live and breathe archery every waking moment of their lives and may even be thinking about it when they're sleeping. They are continuously thinking of ways to make themselves better. They think of future events and what they will need to do to achieve their goals. Each archer has the final say as to what he will do and how he will do it.

Practice is an important part of preparing to compete, but we all practice. Excellent archers are continually preparing for the next event, *even while competing in events*. The more competitions these archers shoot, the less time they have to actually practice, so competitions become practice. Generally speaking, while average archers become excited and want to do well at these events, it is clear who has the advantage. The top archers perform just as they do in practice; that is, very well. However, most average archers treat competitions as something vastly different from their practice sessions. So, if you want to be competitive, it is important to compete as much as possible. The more competitions you are involved in, the more your practice and competition experiences will be similar.

Another important aspect of preparation is proper use of the imagination. When practicing, it is helpful to imagine that you are at the event, battling top archers. The better you can imagine the situation, the more effective this tool is. Imagining yourself at an event makes it easier for you when the actual event occurs because you have already been there, at least in your mind. You are more comfortable with your environment and less pressured. If you can get photos of the competition site or, better, see it, you will have an easier time filling in the other details and creating accurate images.

Determination and attitude are essential aspects of a strong competitor. If you don't practice with determination, how will you shoot consistently? If you don't practice having a good attitude, how will you generate it during competition? Magically? If a practice session is not going well, treat it as an opportunity to work on your determination and attitude.

Planning to Compete

Failing to plan is planning to fail. This may be trite, but it is also true. You always need a plan to reach your goal. Since you are reading this right now, you probably want to do at least a little bit better than you have been. Most people get to performance plateaus and then stay there for long periods. As a result, they get frustrated, and their scores drop. When they are able to work their way back up to their former plateau, they are happy. This is not progress. It is hard to move above and beyond your plateaus unless you develop a plan to work your way off of it.

The first step toward crafting a good plan is understanding your form and technique. You may need a coach to help you along; if a coach is too hard to find or too expensive, then a video camera and a friend, spouse, or parent can help you develop the technique you need.

The next step is to write down your plan as specifically as you can. Writing down what you plan to do and how you plan to do it is so much more powerful than just telling yourself mentally. Start with your goals for the short term and the long term (I will place in the top 10 at the JOAD National Tournament in July). Include physical training routines in your schedule (see chapter 5). Include mental training exercises (see chapter 6). Include coaching sessions, competitions, everything you can think of. Learn about your eating habits and know what sits well with you during competition. (When your stress level is elevated, the foods you are normally comfortable with could turn out to be a major problem. Yes, you have to get to this level of detail.) Practice needs a plan. Each competition needs a plan. Each year needs a plan, and if your goals are lofty, you might need a multiyear plan to reach them!

Putting Your Plan Together

Putting all of this together is not as difficult as it sounds. Good time management is important for all top competitors. Sitting down and writing out everything you need to do and how much time you need to spend on each session is one of your first steps. Then, blending it in with all of your other responsibilities will take a little creativity on your part. Figure 1.1 shows an example of a daily plan

FIGURE 1.1   COMPETITION TIMELINE

Day One/Day Three

6:00 A.M.
Alarm goes off. Mental imagery for 15 minutes before you get out of bed.

6:15 A.M.
Get up and stretch for running.

6:30 A.M.
Take a 30-minute jog/run.

7:00 A.M.
Cool down and stretch.

7:15 A.M.
Practice shooting for one hour.

8:15 A.M.
Get ready for work.

8:45 A.M.
Go to work.

9:00 A.M.
Work

12:00 P.M.
At lunch take a 15-minute mental imagery practice session.

12:30 P.M.
Work

5:00 P.M.
Home from work

5:15 P.M.
Practice for 30 minutes to one hour.

6:15 P.M.
Dinner

7:00 P.M.
The rest of the evening is free time or family time.

10:00 P.M.
Time for bed. Before going to sleep, take 15 minutes for mental training.

Day Two/Day Four

6:00 A.M.
Alarm goes off. Mental imagery for 15 minutes before you get out of bed.

6:15 A.M.
Get up and stretch for weightlifting.

6:30 A.M.
Take 30 minutes for aerobic lifting (light weights, lots of repetitions).

7:00 A.M.
Cool down and stretch.

7:15 A.M.
Practice shooting for one hour.

8:15 A.M.
Get ready for work.

8:45 A.M.
Go to work.

9:00 A.M.
Work

12:00 P.M.
At lunch take a 15-minute mental imagery practice session.

12:30 P.M.
Work

5:00 P.M.
Home from work

5:15 P.M.
Practice for 30 minutes to one hour.

6:15 P.M.
Dinner

7:00 P.M.
The rest of the evening is free time or family time.

10:00 P.M.
Time for bed. Before going to sleep, take 15 minutes for mental training.

to help you make a plan of your own. This is just an example of how you can squeeze in the couple of extra hours it takes to get to a higher level. Keep track of your work and modify it to fit your lifestyle. A measure of your determination to achieve a higher level is the amount of dedication you give to your plan. Making adjustments takes a little time, but eventually you will have everything down to a science as to how much time you plan to give and why.

Although setting a plan and making all the preparations may appear to be hard, it is only half as hard as staying with the plan and improving it. Most people do not have the drive to achieve this level, which is why champions are very rare and highly respected. As Thomas Jefferson once said, "I am a great believer in luck, and I find the harder I work, the more I have of it."

Why Compete?

Why compete? Only you can answer the question. The best answers always seem to include what you learn about yourself while competing. So, why do you? Take a moment and think about it.

Even if your competition is only with yourself in the privacy of your backyard, this book should give you the insight, and we hope the inspiration, to improve.

2

Advanced Form for Recurve Archers

Good shooting technique is built from the ground up. This chapter discusses shooting technique, covering each component from the feet up. We will break down every part of the shot so that you can build a strong, consistent shot from the parts, no matter what conditions you face.

Choosing a Stance

A strong shot begins with the ground you stand on and the way you stand on it. Let's take a look at stances.

Square Stance

For most archers the square stance is best. Everybody is different and every stance is unique, but the square stance is the one to begin with because it helps you find your own stance. The advantage of the square stance is that it automatically aligns the shoulders with the target. By having the shoulders already in line with the target, you will have a natural body alignment from the start (see figure 2.1).

Don Rabska

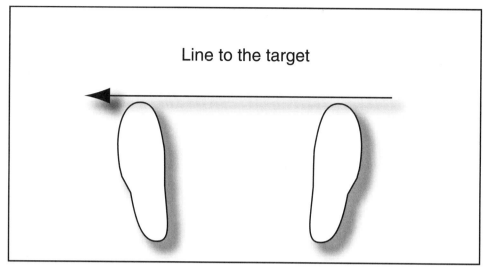

Figure 2.1 Like a baseball batter facing a pitcher, in a square stance your feet form a line pointing straight at the target.

Open Stance

Many advanced archers use an open stance, in which the rear foot is slightly (or more than slightly) ahead of the front foot. This stance allows some archers to "feel" their back muscles better. Many think it offers more stability in windy conditions. You must be cautious, however, not to "open" your chest toward the target, because this will affect alignment. When using an open stance, rotate your upper torso so that it is 90 degrees from the target, as would be the case with the square stance (see figure 2.2).

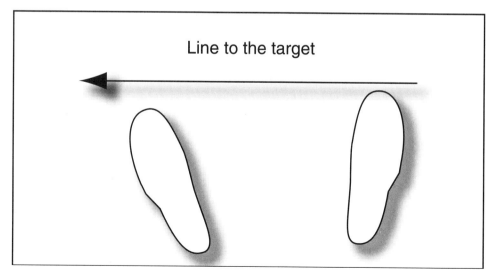

Figure 2.2 In an open stance your target side foot is placed back from the target line, thus "opening" your body to the target slightly.

Good alignment is having your bow hand and the tops of your shoulders in line with the target as shown in figure 2.2. This develops lines of force that are directed toward and away from the target. Develop these lines of force to be as close as possible to the body. The closer these lines are to being directly toward and away from the target, the better your shot consistency will be. Think of the ideal force line as an imaginary line emanating from the center of the target, through your bow arm and shoulders.

Taking Your Stance

Your feet should be at least shoulder-width apart, with approximately 60 to 70 percent of your weight placed on the balls of your feet. Having a slight heel on your shoes will help. Flat shoes that do not have some rise in the heel tend to place the weight on your heels. Placing your weight on your heels will impair your balance and may produce weak shots. This is due to a natural tendency to fall backward when drawing through the clicker. If this occurs, it will be more difficult to continue a smooth, continuous draw, creating a weak shot and resulting in low left arrows (for right-handed archers; the opposite for left-handed archers). Remember, it does not matter whether you shoot an open stance or a traditional square stance. The important considerations are comfort and stability.

Leg Placement

You should distribute weight evenly on both of your legs, and they should be relaxed. Leg strength in archery is as important as upper-body and midsection strength and possibly more important since your legs are responsible for your overall stability and balance. If your desire is to be a top archer, develop good leg strength. Your knees should be relaxed but not locked. Locking your knees will restrict blood flow, make you less stable, and raise your center of gravity, not to mention waste precious energy.

Hip and Abdomen Placement

Your hip position works to stabilize your body. To find the correct hip position, take your shooting stance with your feet about shoulder-width apart. Next, tilt your buttocks up (that is, tilt your rear up and then relax, allowing your hips to tilt forward into a natural relaxed position). Try this several times to get the feel of relaxing so that your hips set into that natural pocket. Do not force your hips forward, but they should be under you. Tightening the lower part of your abdomen below your navel will pull your hips into the correct position automatically (see figure 2.3).

Once you find your natural relaxed position, you are ready to focus on some of the more key points in the shooting technique. While in this position, focus on tightening your abdomen about 3 inches (7.5 centimeters) below your navel. Tighten your abdomen slightly as if you were going to get punched, but do not

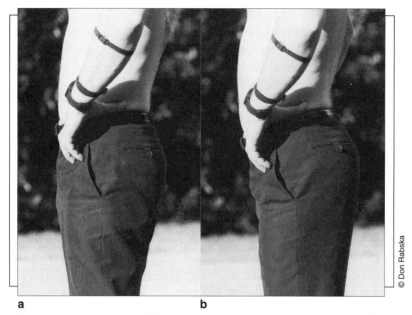

© Don Rabska

a   b

Figure 2.3 From a natural stance *(a)* tilt your hips forward *(b)*. This position stabilizes your whole shot.

pull your abdomen inward in an attempt to look a few pounds thinner. Now, relax every part of your body except the abdomen, while at the same time maintaining good body posture (no slouching). Allow everything to relax down to that area of the abdomen. This technique will connect your legs, midsection, and upper body into one unit instead of three independent parts. By relaxing, it will also lower your center of gravity, making you very stable with greatly improved balance. You must maintain the slight tightness in your abdomen throughout the entire shot. It will take some practice, but if you do it right, your bow sight movement will be reduced significantly.

You will find that aiming is easier and you will develop extra strength in your shot when you tighten your abdomen. Additionally, tightening your abdomen will keep your ribs down so that you will not have a tendency to arch your back. This is a more common problem among women, but many men have a tendency to do this as well. This technique will also improve your shooting by reducing body movement caused by wind.

Taking Up the String

Many archery books advocate placing the string in the first finger joints of the drawing hand. The method recommended here shows the string placement between the first and second joints. This positioning is important because of the biomechanics necessary to comfortably hold the string in the hand while keeping the fingers as relaxed as possible. Placing the string in the first joints increases the load on the flexor muscles (the muscles used for closing your hand) of the drawing arm and makes achieving a relaxed release more difficult.

When taking a grip or hook on the string, try to keep your draw hand relaxed, using only enough strength to hold the string in its position without your fingers slipping. Keep this feeling through the entire drawing process. Also, when drawing the bow, keep your fingers vertical to the string. The vertical position of the fingers at full draw is very important for horizontal grouping control.

Another consideration is how much pressure is placed on each finger. Virtually all top archers place the majority of the bow's draw weight on the middle finger, typically about 60 percent of the string pressure. However, the pressure placed on the first and third fingers can vary significantly partly because of shooting style but also because of the physical differences in archers' hands. The physical differences in the length of your fingers may require more or less pressure on the top or third finger. The only common attribute is that your middle finger is longer than your first and third fingers. There is a common physical difference: In about 70 percent of the population, women's first (index) fingers are longer than their third fingers, whereas men are usually the opposite, having third fingers that are longer than their index fingers.

A basic guideline would be to place 60 percent of the string pressure on your middle finger, 25 percent on your third finger, and 15 percent on your top finger. Using too much top finger will force the third finger off the string and create more tension in the flexor muscles. However, feeling these exact percentages is very difficult. A better approach is to try for a feel of equal pressure on all three fingers and let your hand find a natural balance in the amount of pressure on each finger.

Positioning Your Bow Hand

Your bow hand should be positioned so the knuckles are at approximately 45 degrees to the vertical (see figure 2.4). This position keeps the grip pressure on the thumb pad of the hand, located directly between the joint of the thumb (the joint closest to the palm) and the "lifeline" of the palm. This position allows your bow arm elbow to be rotated out more easily (for better bone alignment) and the line of force of the draw to run along the radial bone of the bow arm. This does not

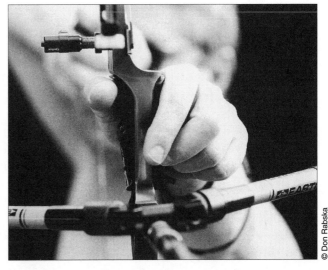

© Don Rabska

Figure 2.4 The bow rests on the pad of your thumb, along your lifeline. The entire bow hand is completely relaxed.

mean that slight modifications of this position are wrong; this is just the recommended position for the majority of archers and usually the best biomechanical location.

Maintaining a relaxed bow hand is important as well. Any tension above what is needed to keep your hand stable may torque (twist) the bow, usually resulting in left arrow impacts (the opposite for left-handed shooters). Also, it is easier to consistently reproduce relaxation than tension. A bow grip that allows for a relaxed bow hand position throughout the shot will produce the most consistent results. The bow must be allowed to perform undisturbed. Your bow grip must allow you to have exactly the same bow hand position on every shot, and must also allow for this relaxed position under any physical or environmental conditions.

Positioning Your Shoulders

Your bow arm and drawing arm scapula (shoulder blade) positions are most important. As your stance sets the foundation for your body, the scapulas set the foundation for the shot. If the scapulas are not in the correct position (down), the rest of your form will not be stable. Do not arch your back or move your shoulders back; instead, raise your head and sternum *straight* up, moving the scapulas (shoulder blades) *straight* down.

While holding the scapulas in a down position, practice raising your arms directly up to your sides, level with the tops of your shoulders, making a T shape. Practice this many times while watching yourself in a mirror to see that your shoulders stay down while raising your arms. To help achieve the correct scapula position, imagine that a string tied to the very top of your chest (sternum) is attached to a helium balloon, making you raise your head and sternum *straight* up (being cautious not to arch your back). If done correctly, the scapulas will go down. This is the shoulder, or scapula, position you want to develop for your shooting technique. This scapula position is the most important part of the shot for overall stability and consistency. This is actually your *true anchor* and will be the basis for determining your true draw length.

For the bow arm shoulder, reach your bow arm down along your leg as if your pockets have been lowered and you are reaching for your last coins. Another description is to move your bow arm straight down (with your palm flat against your leg), reaching until the shoulder stops in a natural position without undue effort. From this position, rotate the upper portion of your bow arm in slightly until the arm rotation comes to a natural stop, but do not force it beyond this point. When you raise your bow arm, keep the scapula down and raise only the arm. When raised, the inside crease of the elbow joint will be vertical. This will align the bones at the shoulder joint, giving you bone-to-bone alignment.

Bone-to-bone alignment at the shoulder joint offers the most rigid resistance possible to the recoil of the bow. A bow, like a gun, recoils on release. The bow goes forward only when the arrow has completely separated from the bowstring. For some, raising only the arm will take a good deal of practice. Again, it is best to practice in front of a mirror with your shirt off so you can easily see your shoulder position. When done properly, the top of the shoulder joint should create a V shape (see figure 2.5). This V location is at the connection of the arm and shoulder. Also, if the shoulder position is correct, the palm of your hand should be facing the ground with your hand fully open as shown. As you curl your fingers, you will see that your knuckles will form a natural 45-degree angle, automatically placing your bow hand in the proper position.

Your drawing arm scapula must also be down and equal in height to the bow arm scapula. This is necessary for the drawing arm scapula to have full range of motion. Raising the drawing arm scapula even slightly will greatly limit your range of motion in the scapula, usually forcing some arm use to control the draw.

© Don Rabska

Figure 2.5 Raising your arm but not your shoulder creates a telltale V-shaped notch at the top of your shoulder

Positioning Your Bow Arm

Many archers use the muscles of their bow arm shoulders to maintain bow arm position and stability. This works to some degree, but not well over long shooting sessions. The most efficient way to develop power to the bow arm is to use the tendons under the arm and have bone-to-bone alignment. When raising the bow arm, reach toward the target, but reach from under the arm, not from the muscles (deltoids) at the top of the shoulder. To do this correctly, your bow arm and bow arm scapula must be in the correct position. When you reach from underneath the arm, you should feel some discomfort as you reach toward the target (without a bow in your hand). The feeling of discomfort will extend from approximately the armpit to the elbow, but don't worry; that is the proper sensation. When shooting, the discomfort is eliminated by the force of the bow pushing toward you. If the reach is done properly, the shoulder will actually drop more (slightly), increasing shoulder stability and improving bone alignment because of the activation of the "lats" (latissimus dorsi muscles). Try to relax the muscles on the top of your shoulder and reach from underneath. The use of the tendons in this method of reaching can allow you to "stretch" forward toward the target. If you try to reach toward the target with the muscles of the shoulder, the bow arm is virtually static unless the scapula is raised, which is incorrect.

Executing the Predraw

The predraw allows for a moment of preparation before the shot. That is, it allows you to run a quick checklist of all of the previously discussed components that make up the shot. For example, you can run through an almost instant list of how each body position feels. You can make certain that your bow hand and drawing fingers are relaxed, your scapulas are down, your stance feels stable, your alignment is correct, and so on. More important, it offers the opportunity for you to take a partial draw until the drawing elbow is about 90 degrees to the back (see figure 4.1d on page 45).

This position allows you to draw the bow with the muscles attached to your scapula rather than with your arm. If the draw is started from brace height and continues to full draw, there has to be a point of muscle transition at which the tension goes from the biceps to the scapula. With a predraw, you can actually stop at this point to allow your biceps to relax so the muscle load is shifted to your scapula. At the predraw position it is also possible to correct any misalignments. If you draw the bow directly from brace height, you must develop alignment as part of the draw by rotating your chest 90 degrees from the target while drawing. Drawing directly from brace height without stopping does not allow much time to make all the necessary body adjustments for a well-executed shot.

In the predraw, the distance your drawing hand is pulled back can range from about the shoulder joint of the bow arm to very close to full draw. The position you choose depends on what works and feels best to you. Whichever position you choose, the drawing arm forearm should be somewhere between the jaw and the forehead in height. Find the location that best allows you to feel a direct line to the drawing arm scapula and then be consistent in your forearm placement in the predraw. Remember to fully relax the biceps of the drawing arm in the predraw. Relaxing the drawing hand and forearm will also assist greatly in relaxing the biceps and allow the proper use of the scapula. Realize that power comes from relaxation, not tension.

Stabilizing the Shoulder

The bow arm reach should be performed while maintaining a balance in energy between the bow arm and drawing arm when coming to predraw—that is, reaching toward (bow arm) and drawing away (drawing arm) from the target at the same moment so that both halves of your body maintain balance (harmony).

Having the drawing arm scapula in the down position will also create a shorter, more efficient follow-through. When the draw is executed correctly, the drawing hand should come only to the neck on release rather than to the shoulder as was taught for many years (see figure 2.6). With the drawing arm scapula in the down position, the drawing hand cannot travel past the neck on release, biomechanically speaking. To have your release hand travel farther than the neck, the drawing arm scapula must be raised, allowing the arm to hinge at the shoulder rather than using the entire shoulder as a single unit. Many archers raise the drawing shoulder as soon as they prepare for the draw or predraw. Raising the drawing arm scapula to initiate the draw does not allow the drawing shoulder to be placed in the most efficient position for optimum scapula motion (also known as "back tension") or for a full range of motion. If your drawing scapula is raised, there is a tendency in the full draw position to "stall" or to have difficulty drawing through the clicker (the final motion of the draw just before release). Additionally, it can cause the drawing elbow to be too far outside of "line" to

© Don Rabska

a   b   c

Figure 2.6 From full draw *(a)* the string hand flies back upon release *(b)*, but only to the neck even through the follow-through *(c)* and not onto the shoulder as has been taught in the past.

allow for the best possible draw force line alignment. It is your scapula position that provides good drawing alignment, allowing your elbow to be aligned with the arrow rather than outside the arrow line. Having both scapulas down and level is critical to having good shoulder stability.

Aligning the Shot

There is no physical reason that 98 percent of all archers cannot get "in line"—in other words, getting the drawing elbow directly (or very nearly) in line with the arrow. Many archers are stuck with the belief that their arms are too short to achieve good line, so they compensate by using an extreme side anchor (which creates left shots for a right-handed archer, the opposite for a left-handed archer). The only reason that archers cannot obtain good line is improper positioning of the drawing arm shoulder or scapula. Archers who use their biceps muscles to draw the bow will often have this problem. When using your arm to draw the bow, your entire shoulder unit is kept forward. "Arm shooters" will often slouch at the shoulders as well, thus preventing good use of the back.

Many coaches tell their archers to use their backs, but do not really say how to do that. The process is really very simple. If the drawing arm biceps are relaxed, the only way to draw the bow is with the muscles attached to the scapula of the drawing arm. Additionally, the forearm of the drawing arm should be placed within a specific range as noted in the predraw section to develop good scapula motion. Maintain the relaxed drawing arm biceps when starting the final draw from the predraw position. Keep this relaxed feeling during the final draw process.

Always keep in mind that good shooting technique is, in fact, good posture. If you slump or slouch at the shoulders, the road to success in archery is not going to be an easy one. It will be an uphill ride, and you will be very slow in reaching your desired destination. On the other hand, if you use good posture and good bone alignment, the road to success will be a smooth highway with few bumps. Using your bone structure is one of the key factors of being able to shoot consistently all day long. If you do not align your skeleton (bone alignment) to take up the pressures involved, you will have to rely on your muscles, ligaments, and tendons to control the shot. Muscles fatigue rapidly and therefore so does the quality of the shot. Good bone alignment will allow you to use only the muscles necessary for good shot execution. Excessive muscle use only leads to a loss of power and body stability through fatigue.

Your shooting technique must have a strong foundation. Body and bone alignment are critical to maintaining shot consistency from arrow to arrow. To shoot consistently for an entire day, you must be relaxed.

Positioning Your Head

Your head should be turned as far toward the target as possible without overstressing your neck. The more directly you can face the target, the better line you will produce and the clearer your sight picture will be. This is quite necessary if you wear glasses when you shoot. To see out the sighting eye lens, you must have your head turned well toward the target. If your head is turned away from the target, this undermines good line and moves the bowstring farther from your chest, resulting in a greater tendency to collapse on the shot. The farther the line of force is moved away from the shoulders, the greater the tendency to collapse.

There are as many shapes of the human face as there are people. Fortunately, most head and face shapes and necks fall into a few categories. Some people have an "archer's face," with nose and chin lengths that allow their head position to be very natural and to face the target directly. Other archers will need to compensate for their facial features. For example, some archers have short noses, causing them to tilt their head well forward to touch their nose on the string. If you have a short nose, you may use a kisser button as a "nose" button to help avoid tilting your head too far forward. An anchor more to the side of your chin can help this situation as well, but be careful not to go past the corner of your chin at anchor.

Finding Your True Anchor

The anchor is commonly described in most archery instruction books as a spot (usually on the face) where archers draw the bowstring to develop a consistent draw position. This description is not really the true anchor, but more accurately the "rear sight" position. The true anchor is actually the position of the two scapulas because good bone alignment must be maintained to develop a truly consistent draw position. If you use your head as your anchor, your head can "float" into different positions—forward to meet the string, down, or to one side. Using only the head as the anchor is the most common cause of inconsistency in shooting form. When archers get tired, they often move their heads forward to meet the string. This, of course, results in a shortened draw. Some tiring archers tilt their heads down. This not only affects their string alignment by forcing them to see the bow sight from a different position but also causes their shoulders to slump or "round," greatly reducing their ability to use their backs properly. If the scapulas are properly set and used to "feel" the full draw position, then the draw can be very consistent from shot to shot. This way your head is used as a rear sight simply to obtain an accurate and consistent sight picture. The scapula position, not the face or chin, is where the true anchor is created. Your body knows from your scapula positions where to draw every time. If you maintain the same feeling of the draw from start to follow-through, then the first 20 inches of the draw will feel no different from the last quarter inch of the draw. The real key to good shooting is to keep moving and just try to get the sight somewhere near the bull's eye by the time the clicker goes off.

Stabilizing Your Draw

Some archers have tremendous shaking problems. When they come to full draw, their bow arms shake excessively or their drawing arms shake almost uncontrollably. This condition is almost always caused by a "point of instability." In other words, an unstable muscle group usually causes the severe shaking experienced by most of these archers. The most common causes are excessive tension in the drawing arm biceps or misalignment of the bow arm. An incorrect bow arm scapula position is the second most common cause of this instability. However, it is worth noting that the point of instability is not necessarily localized in the area of the most severe shaking. For example, tightness in the drawing arm biceps may be the cause of excessive bow arm shaking, while the drawing arm appears stable. To correct this condition, you must isolate the muscle group that is causing the problem. Next, relax that specific muscle group and possibly reposition that part of the body into a better biomechanical position.

The drawing hand too must be relaxed to achieve a good release of the string. The best release comes from relaxation. At the moment the clicker signals the release, the fingers of the drawing hand should fully relax and the draw continue. The shot does not stop when the clicker clicks, and the draw must be continued as if nothing had changed. The only change is the fact that you are no longer holding the string. Many archers relax their entire drawing shoulder when releasing. This action creates a collapse of the shot, or more accurately, a collapse of the drawing shoulder, creating a "soft" shot. The ideal release is achieved by relaxing only the fingers of the drawing hand to create the release. The drawing arm continues as if you were still drawing the arrow through the clicker. Obviously, the release hand reacts to the looseness of the string and moves rapidly back, creating the follow-through. Think of the follow-through and not the release. If you think of the release, you will tend to "stop" the shot to release and then "fake" the follow-through. Think of only relaxation while continuing the draw to create a smooth but aggressive follow-through action, producing a virtually pause-free release.

As I mentioned, I recommend that you take a fairly deep grip on the bowstring. Most elite archers start with the bowstring placed between the first and second joints of the middle finger. Archers using this grip should use a finger separator (can't pinch) on the finger tab. Shooting with the string in the first joints or on the fingertips will often create sore fingers as well. This is the result of increased friction because your tensed fingers will not open easily to release the string. A deeper grip allows greater relaxation in your forearm, allowing the flexor muscles of your arm to relax. It will also give you greater control of the bowstring.

To release the string, you need only complete the relaxation of the drawing hand and forearm. You will find that your fingers will not get as sore (the source of any remaining soreness will be string pressure, not friction), and you will maintain a very relaxed position all the way to the end of the follow-through.

Shooting As One Motion

Archers who use their scapulas to draw the bow will come through the clicker very easily and with a smooth, constant motion. Arm shooters will struggle because of the conflicting forces of the biceps muscles and the muscles attached to the scapulas. This action will cause their arrows to move back and forth through the clicker as if they were trying to saw their arrow rests in half. Continuous motion during the shot is vital for top performance. When coming to anchor, be mindful of keeping the drawing arm biceps relaxed so as not to create a static or frozen hold in an attempt to find the correct string location on your chin. Coming to anchor is a critical point in your technique. You need to maintain the feeling in your back while drawing the string to your chin. It is perfectly acceptable to slow down as you approach your anchor, but do not stop completely or change the direction of the draw in order to anchor. Remember, your face or chin is not really the anchor; it is simply the rear sight.

Continuing Through

Continuing through a shot warrants great attention and is critical to the development of a well-executed shot. Motion, or more accurately, momentum, is the basis for creating consistent energy or power from the bow. The most critical time in the shot is that one second just before, during, and after the loose of the bowstring. However, the most critical element in the shot is determined by the direction of force in which sufficient momentum is created at the moment of release. In other words, the string must be released from the farthest point of the draw while in motion. There can be no forward motion of the drawing fingers, only backward motion and relaxation of the drawing hand while maintaining motion in the scapula. If your shot motion is stopped in an effort to release the string, your drawing hand fingers and string will roll forward away from your face (toward the target) before losing contact with the finger tab. This will reduce the energy from the bow and change the position of the bowstring at release, commonly resulting in left or low left arrow impacts (for right-handed archers, the opposite for left-handed archers). If you have ever witnessed "flight" competition, you will quickly understand this concept. To achieve the greatest power from their bows, flight shooters draw and quickly release while in the motion of the draw.

When you release the bowstring properly and cleanly at maximum tension, you absorb virtually none of the bow's energy, an experience known as the *jolt*. The jolt occurs only when the bow's full energy is unleashed on the arrow. The residual effect causes the body to recoil from the instantaneous transfer of energy, thus negatively affecting the shot. This body reaction is quite noticeable in many of the world's elite archers.

Reviewing the Critical Components

In review, good archery technique and proper bone alignment are necessary to maintain good control of motion. To develop correct scapula motion (back tension), you must relax the drawing arm biceps. When you do, the drawing arm scapula will automatically move toward the spine and bring the draw elbow into alignment. Pay close attention to placing the drawing arm forearm somewhere between your mouth and your forehead during the draw. You must find the elbow location that best allows you to feel a direct line to the drawing arm scapula. This position is critical in making the draw "direct" without creating additional muscle activity in the drawing arm shoulder. When the drawing arm position is correct, the draw will feel very natural, as though arm and scapula were fused together like a long lever. Relaxing the drawing hand and forearm will also assist in good scapula motion and in achieving a relaxed release.

Continuous motion is undoubtedly one of the key components to achieving top performance. When the lines of forces are directly toward and directly away from the target, and are maintained throughout the shot, little can go wrong. The launch and flight path of the arrow will remain undisturbed. Having momentum in a positive direction will create consistency and the reproducibility needed for every shot.

Think of the shot as completing a circle, where the beginning and end meet. Also, think of the draw as the shot, because there is no shot without the draw. This may seem obvious at first, but it is actually more complex than first appearances would indicate. The draw is everything to the shot because the lines of force are determined by the way we draw the bow and retain continuity of the draw. The most crucial part of the draw is the anchor because we often err by stopping to anchor. Anchoring like this often causes an abrupt change in the directions of force. When we stop the draw for any reason, momentum is halted and the lines of forces (force vectors) change drastically.

The shot must be a single action once you have initiated the draw; you should never actually stop, *especially* when the clicker clicks. The clicker should only indicate to your subconscious mind the signal to complete the final degree of relaxation in the draw fingers. The fact that the draw fingers no longer hold the string is inconsequential to the continuous draw of the bowstring. Again, think of the follow-through and not the release. Focusing on the release can create a desire to stop the draw motion to release the string. The release must be a by-product of the continuous drawing action. The shot cannot be stopped to release the string, as it would constitute a secondary action (a break in the circle), allowing changes in the direction of force while totally eliminating momentum.

Think of the draw as a runaway train on a straight track. The train has tremendous momentum along a straight line. To cause any deviation along that line of force is virtually impossible. Even if you feel that your release is slightly rough, the arrow will, more frequently than not, go to the desired point of impact. When the drawing arm force is generated in a single direction, any secondary influence to that direction will have little to no effect. However, should the motion stop to release the shot, or the lines of forces change due to a transfer of muscle activity into muscles other than the ones required to draw the bow (for example, when anchoring), the shot is easily disrupted. To restart the motion and recreate the original momentum takes much more energy than simply continuing the draw along a straight line. In no other sport does motion stop to complete an action. Hitting a tennis ball, swinging a golf club, throwing a ball, all have continuous motion. Why would our sport be any different? Stopping the draw motion is the most common and devastating error in good archery performance.

Approaching the anchor point (rear sight position) is the most critical step in the draw. If you treat the act of anchoring simply as the rear sight position, this mental picture may help you maintain a consistent draw and not treat the anchor as a totally separate event in the shot process. The drawing hand should be brought into the face with consistent placement, but not hard against the face because nerve receptors are very sensitive to pressure. It is better not to "anchor hard." When coming into anchor, initiate a light touch; then move into a "snug" anchor while still maintaining slow, continuous motion. The draw can remain at the same speed or even speed up if the muscle activity remains in the muscles connected to the scapula. If the anchor is hard against the face, the feel of the hand position will be less accurate because of nerve receptor overload. It is easier to feel a light touch in an exact location than hard pressure.

© Human Kinetics

An archer's anchor point is one of the most important steps in executing a proper draw.

The most important part of the shot cycle is the control of momentum in the last fraction of draw. You must give this top priority. You will greatly improve your shot consistency and accuracy if you maintain motion. To accomplish this, focus on what it *feels* like to draw the bow. Maintain this feeling as you approach your rear sight position (anchor), and maintain the same feeling of the draw while positioning the drawing hand under your chin. The draw should not be too fast because this too can create a tendency to stop suddenly. As your drawing hand settles into the rear sight position, the draw can slow down, but you must maintain the draw feeling in your back. As you bring the bow sight near the center of the target, you can increase the speed of the motion slightly or stay at the same velocity, as long as there is no change in the feeling of the draw.

Additionally, give yourself lots of "running room." For example, some archers will try to attain a "set draw" that places the arrow point only a few millimeters from the edge of the clicker. Then the archer has only a small distance to come through the clicker. This does work for some, but for many archers it is not a practical approach to shooting a strong, consistent shot. In this case, archers often stop the draw to cautiously "set up" in preparation of the shot. The problem is that many archers try to hold the draw at that critical location, shifting focus from their backs to their arms without realizing it. This usually causes them to "freeze up" on the target, which then requires them to expend tremendous energy to draw the bow those last few millimeters. If you give yourself more running room and relax, you will have enough arrow point to draw through the clicker and still have ample time to aim the shot while maintaining a smooth, continuous motion.

Connecting With the Target

You may wonder why the shot is smooth and easy when shooting only a few meters from the target, but lost when going to longer distance. When we shoot close to the target, we can feel the shot easily because most of us are concentrating only on our body, with no connection with the target. When shooting at long distance, we lose that good feeling because the focus changes to the sight and aiming, and the feeling and awareness of our bodies is gone. When this happens, the shot is no longer smooth or fluid. It is difficult to focus on yourself and the target at the same time. The conscious mind can think of only one thing at a time.

In archery, we must focus on the target, not the sight. Aiming in recurve archery must be like aiming in bowling, golf, darts, or throwing a ball. Aiming is done in your subconscious mind while your conscious mind is focused on feeling the action. The feeling of your shot must start at the moment of the draw; it is too late if you wait until the anchor.

Learning to feel your shot starts with learning to feel your body. Practice feeling each part of your form from your feet to your head. Feeling is sensation; it is not thinking about the action, but sensing it. Learn what it feels like instead of focusing on the thought of doing it. This will give the clearest message to your subconscious mind for building the best possible subconscious program. Your shot must have a sequence, and you must repeat each step every time.

When shooting at the target, look at the whole target and feel where you want to hit; that is, look at your point of focus. In windy conditions, this will not be the center of the target. The distance is not important as long as you maintain the "target connection." When shooting close, find arrow holes to look at so the target connection is the same whether you are shooting 3 meters or 90 meters. When you can feel a connection with the target, the sight will find its way to the center (or point of focus). When you have developed this sensation through many hours of practice, your mind will have no thought and will work only in real time through feeling.

Each time you prepare to shoot, place your full effort into the shot. At the moment you start drawing, feel the motion of drawing the bow while intently looking at the target. Feel the motion of your drawing arm scapula and concentrate only on this feeling while looking at the target. Feeling the draw and looking at the target becomes "one thing," not two separate steps. Developing full concentration builds confidence. Confidence comes from knowing what it feels like when your form is correct and knowing you can find that feeling when you want to. The correct feeling is the one that enables you to put an arrow in the center of the target. Immerse yourself in that feeling—no thought, only feeling.

3

Developing Your Compound Archery Form

Larry Wise

Studying the fundamental ingredients of a good archery shot will lead you to conclude that no matter what bow you use, most of the steps involved are the same. Yes, each type of bow requires some different skills to attain maximum consistency and accuracy, but most of the skills will transfer from one type of bow to another. Such is the case with recurve and compound bows.

The most dramatic difference between recurve and compound bows can be experienced in the draw stroke. The recurve bow requires a smooth increase of force from beginning to peak weight at the end. The compound bow, by design, increases to peak weight in the first half of the draw stroke. Following that, the weight on the string reduces by 60 to 70 percent, typically allowing the archer to hold only 15 to 24 pounds at full draw.

As far as your physical form is concerned, shooting the compound bow can be done from a completely stationary full draw position with no arrow movement across the arrow rest. Recurve archers cannot be still at full draw because they are at peak weight, which cannot be sustained for any length of time. So, most recurve archers choose to aim and shoot pulling the arrow through a draw check device known as a *clicker*.

Shooting from a still or static position involves a slightly different strategy from shooting on the move. And since the compound is most often shot with a handheld release aid device, this strategy involves how the archer implements back tension to complete the release of the string. As you read this chapter on shooting the compound bow, please be aware of this difference, but also be sure to note the similarities of the other form steps with those of the recurve bow.

As Bud Fowkes, former Olympic coach, preached for years, archery is a simple two-step sport:

Step One: Learn to shoot a ten.

Step Two: Repeat step one.

This may be oversimplified, but a closer look at one word brings to light how relevant it is. That word is *repeat*. A monkey in a room with a machine gun and a target will eventually shoot a ten. Repeating it on demand is quite another matter. Repeating a shot performance puts the burden on how you learn to do it in the first place.

I believe and teach that building a repeatable archery shot must involve back tension. This chapter outlines how to do that while using a mechanical release aid with the compound bow.

Some Important Concepts

I've taught math for over 30 years. Just as advanced systems of mathematics rely on the basic rules of algebra to complete their high-level calculations, your archery form must rely on the proper use of your body's core, your spine, to complete the shot. This and the knowledge of how to build your form step by step are the only ways to get your extremities functioning on a winning level. Therefore, archery form, like a mathematical system, begins with some definitions of important terms.

Since shooting form is a set of precise movements that must relate to the final outcome, we must first define that final outcome. If our objective is not well defined, to what can we compare each step in order to evaluate its effectiveness? I coach my students to know that in archery shooting form, the final objective is the appropriately timed execution of back tension.

The next logical question is, What is back tension? The term has been used for years without ever being defined, and without a definition, not enough archers have been achieving it. To build good form, you must learn the definition of back tension.

Back tension is the contraction of the dominant or drawing side rhomboid muscles, aided by the levator scapulae muscle, which causes a micro sliding rotation of the scapula toward the spine.

Some other muscles must assist. As the rhomboids contract, the trapezius must also contract to lock the shoulder unit with the scapula and pin them both next to the rib cage.

Now you know the objective of good form. Every time you nock an arrow, every part of your form must be geared to setting up the proper execution of back tension. If not, then whatever it is you're doing is wasting energy or working against your objective.

Do you need to know where these muscles are and their names? I think so. The more you know about your objective, the more likely you will be to achieve it. Figure 3.1 shows the rhomboid and levator scapulae muscles, which must be contracted to move the shoulder blade and shoulder unit toward the spine. It also shows the trapezius and how it performs its function of keeping the shoulder blade close to the rib cage while linking the shoulder unit to it.

A second term that needs attention before starting the form sequence is *full draw position*. I use this term to replace the term *anchor point*. The term *anchoring* creates the counterproductive image of stopping or stillness in archers' minds. As you've read previously, these images are particularly important to avoid when shooting a recurve bow. The term *anchor point* also causes archers to focus on the relationship of their drawing hands to their faces and not on what is happening in their backs and shoulders. Your real anchor happens when your drawing shoulder and scapula attain the position that is most beneficial to the execution of back tension.

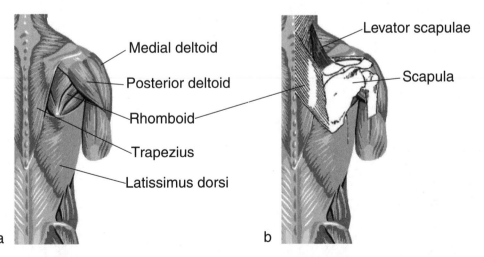

Medial deltoid

Posterior deltoid

Rhomboid

Trapezius

Latissimus dorsi

Levator scapulae

Scapula

a   b

Figure 3.1 The major and minor rhomboid muscles *(a)* link the scapula to the spine area while the levator scapulae muscle *(b)* links the scapula to the base of the skull. When these muscle groups contract, the scapula rotates and slides a small distance toward the spine, creating back tension.

Full draw position is that position to which you draw the bowstring in order to place your spine and scapula in the most effective alignment for executing back tension.

This position has various *secondary* reference points on the face and neck that an archer can use to reinforce the final full draw position. However, primary attention should and must be placed on the location of the drawing side scapula and shoulder unit.

Full draw position is, by definition, the prerequisite of back tension and must also be the focus of each preceding part of the form sequence. Keeping both of these definitions in mind while reading the rest of this chapter will be important to your understanding of each step, as well as the step sequence.

Form Sequence

This section describes 12 form steps and how they relate to one another. As you read them, keep in mind that you must strive to maximize the use of your skeleton while minimizing the use of your muscles. Every step you read follows this principle with the purpose of preparing for the optimum, stationary body position at full draw. In this position, you can use back tension to its fullest potential.

Step 1: The Stance

Every archery shot begins with your stance. For some, this might be in a wheelchair or some other supporting device, but for most of us, it's on two feet. Regardless of your needs for positioning yourself, your stance must provide stability for each shot, be consistent for each shot, and remain constant between shots.

Stance begins with foot position. Feet that are hip- or shoulder-width apart will provide the stability for the upper body. If they're too close together, your body will rock back and forth while you're aiming or in the slightest wind. If they're too far apart, you'll strain your lower back, which in turn will prevent proper use of your back muscles.

Your feet must also be oriented in such a way that you minimize upper-body twist. To accomplish this, place an arrow on the ground or floor pointed toward the target. Your toes should touch this arrow to form an "even" stance. To form an "open" stance, pull your target-side foot one, two, or three inches away from the arrow. This move will open the front of your body toward the target. A closed stance places your other foot several inches away from the line, but is not recommended because of its tendency to inhibit proper back muscle use.

The stance you choose must support your upper body while it prepares, draws the bow, aims, increases back tension, and releases the arrow. Your stance can do this best when your skeleton holds up your body weight. In other words, use only enough muscle to keep your legs straight and relax the rest. Comfort is your best guide for this—if you are not comfortable, you are trying to hold too much weight with muscle.

To determine which stance is the best for you, use the closed eye test. This test involves drawing and aiming an arrow, then closing your eyes for a count of seven or eight. Then open your eyes to notice if you have drifted left or right. Do it again. If you find a pattern after four or five tests, then you should make an adjustment by moving your rear foot in the direction of the drift. This new stance should help dampen your drifting motion. Keep in mind that if you are drifting with your eyes closed, then you are fighting against that drift while you are aiming.

In perfect conditions you should be able to maintain your stance with little difficulty, but in imperfect conditions you must make adjustments. For instance, if you must stand on uphill or downhill slopes, then move your feet closer together to get your heels nearer to the same height. Other possible solutions involve scraping dirt or placing a rock under your downhill foot. Practice these compromises to your best stance so you know what works best for you.

Step 2: The Nock

To maintain focus on the target and correct body alignment to it you should nock every arrow in the shooting plane. In other words, hold your bow in or near to vertical. This will allow you to nock your arrow with no wasted energy, which is important if you intend to shoot a lot of shots.

Moving around while you are nocking an arrow can also get your body out of line with the target. Your stance sets your body to avoid drift, so don't twist out of shape or tense your muscles afterward. Keep relaxed and aligned, and the rest of the shot sequence will flow properly from this simple but necessary form step.

Step 3: The Bow Hand Position

After nocking the arrow, you must position both hands for the rest of the shot sequence. This is one of the most important steps in archery because the launch of the arrow is last affected by the position of the bow as held by the bow hand. If your bow hand is transferring torque to the handle (i.e., twisting it), then the bow is not free to repeat its performance, and you won't be consistent.

To minimize the torque transfer from hand to handle, you must use your hand as a support rod only; gripping is not needed or wanted. Gripping the handle is going to cause torque transfer, whereas keeping your fingers and thumb completely relaxed will not (see figure 3.2).

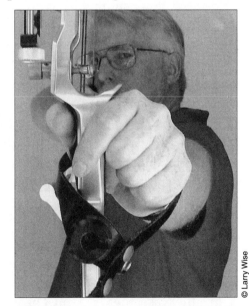

Figure 3.2 Your bow hand should not grip the bow handle. Your fingers must be relaxed and your thumb pointing forward. A relaxed hand will not transfer torque to the bow handle.

The lifeline in your bow hand serves as a dividing line between the usable and unusable parts of your bow hand. Contact between your hand and the grip area of the bow must be limited to the thumb side of the lifeline (see figure 3.3).

Contacting the bow grip with the other part of the palm requires rotating the wrist downward, which puts the forearm in the path of the string. This results in the string hitting the arm for many archers. If your wrist is not rotated down, your knuckles form a 45-degree angle with the bow handle, and your forearm will not move into the path of the string. Most of all, you minimize torque transfer to the handle.

Bow hand placement is where the shot begins and ends. That is to say, the bow hand is the first body part to touch the bow handle and the last body part to be touching it as the arrow crosses the rest. You must get it correct at the first moment of touch and keep it there throughout the shot. This is so important that I require 95 percent of my students to correct this form first.

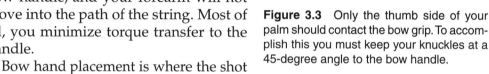

Figure 3.3 Only the thumb side of your palm should contact the bow grip. To accomplish this you must keep your knuckles at a 45-degree angle to the bow handle.

Getting the bow hand in place and relaxed will ensure that no torque will be transferred to the handle during the remainder of the shot. Just think about how many times you've missed left or right, and you'll realize that improving your bow hand placement will make a big difference in your scores. I can't stress enough that the shot begins and ends with the bow hand.

Step 4: The Release Hand Position

Your release, or drawing, hand position must be established with the bow still in the shooting plane. For finger shooters this position involves placing the fingers around the string and learning how to let the string push them out of the way with consistency.

Those archers shooting a release aid need to hook it to the string and position their hands and fingers around the aid. Gripping too tightly will cause unwanted muscle tightness in the hand and forearm. Keep in mind that our desire is to use as little muscle and as much bone structure as possible. Unused muscles can be relaxed; used muscles can't.

In either case, the wrist must be in line with the forearm (see figure 3.4). If it is not, the forearm cannot be relaxed. The hand and forearm must become a straight-line pulling unit while the bow is being drawn. Along with the upper arm, the wrist and forearm act only as a connecting unit between the back/shoulder unit and the fingers once full draw position is reached.

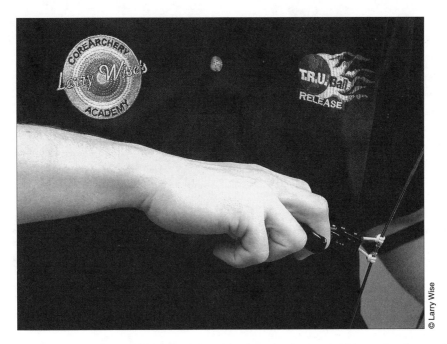

© Larry Wise

Figure 3.4 Hold your release with a straight and relaxed wrist to avoid imparting torque to the bowstring.

A tight release hand can be another cause of left-right misses. Imparting different amounts of wrist torque on the release aid will have an effect on the bowstring. For those of you shooting high letoff on your compound, this small effect on your wrist can have a big effect on a string that has only 15 pounds of force on it. A straight and relaxed wrist will get you the best results.

Step 5: The Posture

If you have maintained good posture during the previous steps, then all that remains is to set your head position for the remaining steps. Good posture means that your shoulders are at the same level and not slumped forward. Your head needs to be held upright as though you are looking straight ahead of your body. Then, with your chin level, shift your head slightly rearward (maybe an eighth of an inch) so that it is directly over the top of your spinal column.

This alignment will bring your shoulders, scapula, head, and neck into the best position to execute back tension. In other words, you have placed your drawing side rhomboid and levator scapulae muscles into the position where they have maximum leverage on your scapula. Maintaining this position is crucial to consistent shooting.

To reinforce this positioning, you can tighten your center of gravity inside your abdomen along with your oblique abdominal muscles along the sides of your midriff (see figure 3.5). This tightening will have a linking effect between the top and bottom of your body, making a solid launching platform. In other words, you've solidified your spinal core from the top of your head to your hips and locked it to your shooting base.

Now, with both hands in position and your body erect, simply turn your head 60 degrees or so toward the target. If you move nothing else, just your head, then your body is in position for the remaining form steps.

Step 6: Raising the Bow

At this point the bow must be presented to the target. To do so, you must raise your bow arm and bow without disturbing the posture already established and without inhibiting what must

Figure 3.5 Before raising your bow, set your shoulders and chin level. Make sure your head is directly over your spine.

follow. Maintaining level shoulder position is a must if you want to preserve maximum leverage for your rhomboid muscles (see figure 3.6).

The bow arm should be raised from the shoulder socket and below; that is, your shoulder should stay level as you raise your arm. If leverage is used from the shoulder unit above the head of the humerus bone, chances are high that your shoulder will rise higher and remain there. Try practicing this without your bow so you get to know what it feels like to lift your arm without raising your shoulder. When you think you are doing it correctly, try it with your bow. Check yourself in a mirror to be sure you are keeping your shoulders level.

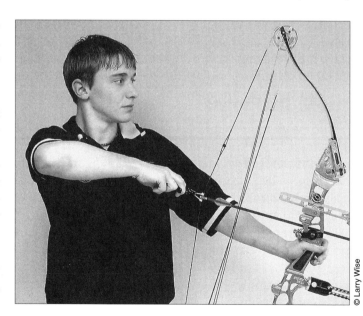

Figure 3.6 Raise your bow with an extended bow arm. Do not raise either shoulder.

Since your release hand is linked to the bowstring, you must raise it along with your bow arm. Raise both arms as a unit. Imagining that your release hand and arm are an extension of the arrow may help you keep it all in line and your shoulders level during the raise.

Many good shooters like to rotate their upper bodies a few degrees toward the target before raising their bows. The purpose is to aid the start of the draw by having the body slightly rotated toward the target. Now when they begin to draw their bow they can use their hips and torso to help draw the bow. This rotation should be done from the hips and must be done before raising the bow.

Step 7: The Draw

When the bow reaches a level slightly higher than the aiming level, the bow hand should be relaxed, the bow shoulder must have remained at its starting level, and the body must be rotated several degrees toward the target (see figure 3.7). Begin drawing the bowstring with the upper body rotating to its starting position and continue the draw with the drawing shoulder unit.

Avoid unnecessary wear and tear on your shoulder. When you start or complete the draw at some level not near the aiming level, you place a high load on your shoulder ball and socket while it is rotating into its final position. Repeated rotation under load is a sure way to incur injury and reduce your longevity in archery. If you can't draw your bow with proper technique, lower the draw weight and shoot a lighter arrow. When done properly, archery is a lifelong enjoyment and not a source of pain and misery.

Drawing should be a smooth operation. You'll need upper and lower drawing arm muscle to begin the draw, but as you pass peak weight, you must relax most of them. By the time you get to full draw position, your biceps and triceps need to be relaxed with the necessary holding force transferred to your back muscles.

Figure 3.7 Raise your bow until you can see your sight just above the middle of the target. Allow the sight to settle to the middle when you get to full draw.

Step 8: The Full Draw Position

You should draw the arrow until you reach your full draw position. This position, as defined earlier, depends on your scapula and drawing shoulder and not on where your drawing hand touches a certain place on your face or jaw. When both shoulders and scapulas have been set in position and prepared to execute back tension, then you are at full draw position.

At this point release shooters stop the draw movement of the arrow. Even though you have stopped moving the arrow across the rest, don't relax any of your rhomboid muscle tension. You must continue increasing back tension throughout the shot sequence; if you stop increasing or, worse yet, decrease tension at full draw, then you have to start the process over again to execute the shot. Rebuilding all that back tension is difficult to do in a timely manner. Once you start it, keep it going until the shot is released.

On the bow arm side, your shoulder has been kept in its level position from the beginning of the draw throughout the aiming and release sequence. In that position the force load of the bow is most consistently transferred into your back through bone structure. If it's raised, muscle must hold that force, which compromises both consistency and stamina.

In full draw position both shoulders are set level with each other, and the bow hand and bow arm muscles are relaxed. The drawing hand wrist is straight and relaxed, as are the forearm and biceps muscles. The drawing side elbow is held level or slightly higher than the shoulders in preparation for final back tension execution (see figure 3.8).

You may establish a touch between your release hand and some part of your face, jaw, or neck, but do not lower your head to meet your hand or the bowstring. This touch is secondary to the proper shoulder position and must not be overemphasized; head and shoulder position are more important.

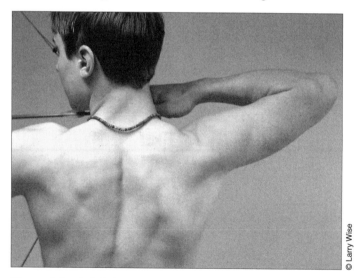

Figure 3.8 At full draw your scapula will be near your spine with space to move closer when you execute back tension.

Step 9: Aiming and Tightening

If you have executed the draw properly, your bow should be pointed slightly high of the target center. Your sight should appear on the upper half of the target. Some prefer it to be at the 11 o'clock position, whereas others prefer the 12 o'clock or 1 o'clock position. Practice whichever you determine to be the best for you.

When you begin on the high side, gravity will help you get the sight down to the middle. Starting low and moving up means you'll have to work against gravity. Back tension, at the very least, must be maintained during target acquisition.

As your sight enters the middle of the target, you should further tighten (contract) your drawing side rhomboid and levator scapulae muscles. This contraction will cause the bottom of your scapula (shoulder blade) to rotate toward your spine. You are now in the midst of your "back tension" shooting objective. This movement is not really visible from the outside, but you can easily feel it and control it.

At the same time you must set into motion all of the actions that will activate your release aid. No matter what kind of release aid you are using, tighten all finger muscles in your release hand as you tighten your back muscles. As your shoulder blade rotates and slides toward your spine, your shoulder unit must move with it. Since your elbow is attached, it too will move slightly (see figure 3.9). Someone can watch for this horizontal movement from behind you to verify that it is happening.

Your drawing side elbow must move in a horizontal plane. It can't move backward (away from the target) because it's attached to your arm and your arm is not going to disconnect from your body. So which way does it move? It moves horizontally at right angles to your arrow and toward your back—in other words, parallel to the shooting line.

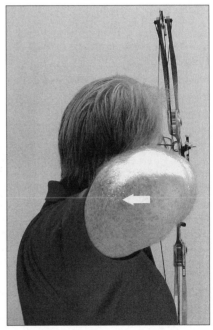

Figure 3.9 When you contract rhomboid muscles your elbow will move to the left as seen in this view. Movement in any other direction can't happen if you are using back tension.

This movement is subtle, but it's there. What can't happen with back tension is elbow movement in the opposite direction. In fact, if your elbow is moving in that direction, your back muscles must be stretching, not contracting (see figure 3.10).

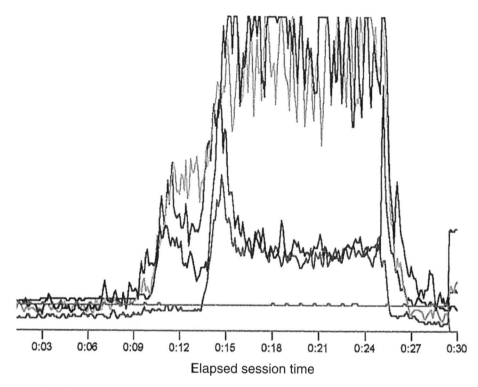

Elapsed session time

Figure 3.10 During a shot sequence I had the activity of four muscle groups monitored in this EMG print out. The top two lines are from the rhomboid and levator scapulae groups that remain highly active until the release. The deltoid and triceps groups show a reduced level of activity after passing peak weight at the 16-second mark and during the aim.

While your back muscles are contracting, your other muscles must remain relaxed. Both forearms and biceps must be relaxed. Your bow hand and fingers must be relaxed also. Now you're ready for the next step.

Step 10: The Release

You must use the subtle movement of the scapula to cause the release to activate in a timely manner. You must also train yourself to maintain release finger tightness while executing back tension because any movement of your elbow will be negated by relaxing your fingers.

During this time, you must be immersed in aiming. Your conscious mind must focus on aiming while your subconscious mind runs back tension execution.

You must not be thinking about activating the release, only aiming. In time, the release activates, sending you to the next step.

Step 11: The Follow-Through

Your back muscles, which have been gradually increasing their tightness just before release activation, will instantly relax when the release occurs. At that instant your release hand will move slightly backward away from the target. If it moves backward violently, then you were using too much arm muscle (see figure 3.11).

Figure 3.11 Your release hand will move back slightly after the release is activated. If it moves back farther (as shown here) you were using too much arm muscle!

Your bow arm should remain out but fall down slightly while your head remains unchanged. Your eyes should remain focused on the target center until the arrow hits it.

Step 12: System Reset

As your muscles relax and you lower your bow, you must give your shot a quick one-second evaluation. Once you've done that, divorce yourself from it. Forget it completely. On your computer you hit CTRL+ALT+DEL when you want to start over, so do that with your mind. Do some relaxation breathing and reach for a new arrow.

Putting It All Together

Use this outline to guide you as you build your shooting form. Each step is critical as it leads to the next and on to the goal of back tension implementation. The best way to do this is to get out a pencil and paper and start writing your own 12 steps. If 12 doesn't suit you, then build what you need.

Writing out your steps is a really important part of understanding how one step relates to and sets up the next. A written list will help you analyze each step and make it fit better in the sequence. Your practice and experimenting tells you *what* to do and *how* to do it; your list determines *when* to do it. Let's face it, doing all the right things the right way won't get you high scores unless you are doing them all at the correct time.

Thinking your way through each step will build the knowledge you need to make quick improvements. Without this written checklist you won't pinpoint that one little flaw that is holding you back from those high scores.

When you find some flaws in your form, fix the one earliest in your list. Shoot at a blank bale without your sight so you can give total mental focus to replacing that flawed step with an improved step. Do this to start and end every practice session until, after 20 sessions, your new form becomes part of your subconscious routine. Once this happens, rewrite your form step list, and remember that your list is always a work in progress.

Form is everything in archery; build it carefully and completely so you know what to do, how to do it, and most important, when to do it.

Shoot straight; keep well.

4

Executing the Shot

Steve Ruis and Claudia Stevenson

Archery is inherently simple—put an arrow on the bowstring, pull the string back, and let go. So, let's not overcomplicate things. But we don't want to oversimplify things either. Is it really that simple? Pull back and let go? Well, the answer is yes and no.

One of the reasons kids and even adult beginning archers often succeed at a high level is just because they don't overcomplicate it. They pull the string back, relax, and let it go. Where we get into trouble is when that isn't good enough, when we want to "get to the next level," or when we decide we want to win and not just have fun. Severe archery troubles, such as target panic, don't happen to beginners because their approach is too simple to mess up. So why complicate things? Because if you don't, you won't be able to compete. All top-level shooters take their shot apart and put it back together.

Two Approaches

Top FITA (Fédération Internationale de Tir à l'Arc, the international archery association) recurve archers talk about "building a strong shot," whereas compound shooters talk about "developing a shot sequence." It sounds like two different approaches to the same thing, executing a shot, but in fact they are the same. For years, the National Archery Association has taught beginning archers the "nine steps to the ten ring." This is a sequence of steps, actually phases, that occurs during a well-executed shot (see figure 4.1, *a-i*). If you ask nonarchers to identify the steps of a shot, though, they will be hard pressed to come up with even two or three steps. This is because to nonarchers

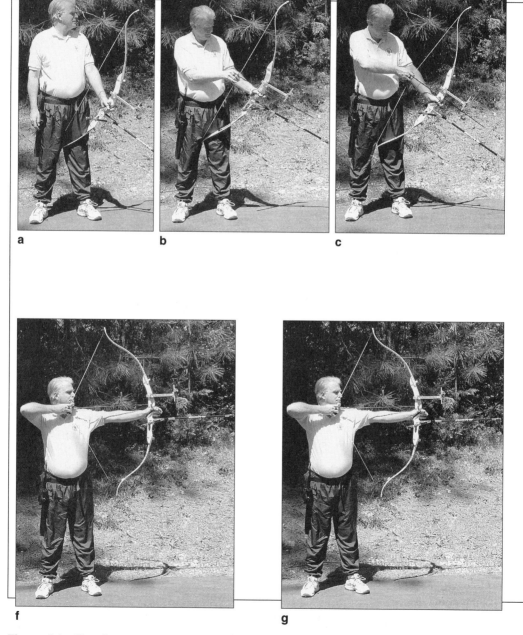

Figure 4.1   The nine steps to the ten ring are: *(a)* stance, *(b)* nock, *(c)* set, *(d)* predraw, *(e)* draw, *(f)* anchor, *(g)* aim, *(h)* release, and *(i)* follow through.
© USA Archery, NADA

it looks like one continuous motion. Relatively speaking, it is, but by breaking it down into steps, you can focus your attention on a particular part of that "one motion shot" when you are practicing or working out a problem in a tournament. It is really hard to work on something if you don't even have a name for it!

d

e

h

i

Top shooters execute shots with what seems like no effort. You have probably heard top athletes complimented with the statement, "She made it look effortless." So, how much work does it take, do you think, to make something look effortless? You got it—a great deal. If you want to be a top archer, you will have to log a lot of time practicing before you can make it look effortless. Even those with the natural talent and natural mental makeup to make a great archer must put in tremendous amounts of time practicing. We know that's not what you wanted to hear. You probably bought this book because you thought just reading it would give you an edge. Sorry to break the bad news to you, but the good news is that in chapter 10 you can learn how to have fun acquiring effortless skill. This chapter is about how to identify what you want to practice.

To be a top shooter, you must execute shot after shot after shot with minimal variation. In FITA rounds you shoot 144 arrows at just four different distances, 36 at each. In field archery, the conditions change much more often. But in any of these competitions, you have to draw the bow and release the arrow in pretty much the same way over and over again. This is why the NFAA's top coach, Bernie Pellerite, says, "Archery is not a sport. It is a discipline!" And he's right.

Repeating something over and over again in exactly the same way is not easy. Ask any basketball player about free throws or golfer about three-foot putts. They'll tell you there is no excuse for missing them—but sometimes it happens. Nobody has ever gotten through an NBA season hitting 100 percent of his free throws. No PGA golfer ever got through a year's tour with no "three putts." But people have gotten close. How was it done? The Greeks knew how when they came up with the saying "Repetition is the mother of learning." So, all you need do is shoot a lot of shots on some regular basis and you will improve? The answer, again, is yes and no. Shooting a lot of practice shots will help. But don't count that one—your mind wandered. And don't count that one—you dropped your bow arm. Don't count that shot—you plucked the string, punched your release . . .You see, if you practice executing bad shots, guess what you are going to get really, really good at.

This chapter will show you how to execute a perfect shot, one you know is in the center before it lands. We know this feeling; you do too. What you want is that feeling on every shot. We won't guarantee that you'll place every arrow in the center, but this is the core of executing perfect shots—a feeling.

We will begin by breaking a shot up into parts. You must examine each part, make it work perfectly, and then practice it until you no longer need to think about it. Only your subconscious mind can make you look effortless.

Building a Shot Sequence (Recurve Shooters)

The photos that show you the "nine steps to the ten ring" are as good a place as any to start if you shoot a recurve bow. How many steps are necessary? The answer depends on a lot of factors, but generally no more or no fewer than this are necessary. Once you have identified all of your phases, elements, or steps, you may find that something got left out, or you may find that one or two steps aren't necessary. Your sequence may change over time and certainly will change when you encounter problems. The key is to *write it down*. Famed archery coach Frank Pearson suggests not only that you write it down, but also that you keep a copy in your quiver and in a practice log. He teaches that if you encounter a problem in a tournament, you need to take the list out during a break and walk through it. Your problem generally has to do with something on that list that you have changed or eliminated.

The nine steps are stance, nock, set, predraw, draw, anchor, aim, release, and follow through. We find just these words to be a little short, so here's our translation:

1. Take your stance
2. Nock an arrow
3. Set your hands
4. Predraw and check
5. Draw the bow
6. Anchor
7. Aim (aim, aim!)
8. Release (let the string go; don't let go of the string)
9. Follow through

Taking Your Stance

Taking your stance means just that. You can review stances in the form chapters, but practicing it can be done anytime. Practice while waiting for a bus or a meeting. Pick a target and take your stance. If your stance is a little bit open one time and a little bit closed the next, you will struggle with consistency. This is one of the greater challenges of field archery. The shooting positions may be slanted uphill, downhill, sideways, or just so irregular that you can't get your normal address of the target. Find your natural stance and then note how your feet and legs are positioned. Then practice getting into your stance.

To check your stance, take it at the practice line, and then draw your bow with your best form *with your eyes closed*. Then open your eyes. If you and your bow aren't facing the target exactly, move your feet so you are and try again. When you are in your best stance, you will be pretty much on target when you open your eyes. Try this at the beginning of your practice sessions. Can you get your stance right away? If not, how many practice shots does it take you to get warmed up and on target? This might be useful to know come tournament day.

Nocking an Arrow

Although this seems blatantly obvious, it's not. Is the cock vane properly positioned? Is the nock up against the nocking point indicator? Has your bottom nock slipped? Did the nock slide all the way onto the string? All of this requires attention at first. Later your subconscious mind will take over, and when you are nocking an arrow, something will *feel* wrong. When you look closer, you will see a broken nock, a frayed serving, a slipped nocking point indicator, or whatever. None of your steps is trivial. Dave Cousins reportedly lost an NAA field championship because of an unobserved broken nock on a single shot.

Setting Your Hands

This means set your bow hand and your string hand. Your bow hand must be set into the riser in the same way for each shot. Your string fingers must similarly be set on the string. You can practice just this, but it is recommended that you follow this with a predraw because that step is designed to check all of the prior steps. If you are a finger shooter—compound or recurve—and you haven't read Don Rabska's piece on the release, run (don't walk) to chapter 2 and read it!

Predraw

The term *predraw* is not actually accurate since it requires starting the draw and then stopping short. It isn't before the draw, as the *pre* would suggest. All you have to do is pull back enough so that you feel pressure in both hands and then you check. Everything. Does your bow hand feel right? Is the target in the right place (not that it will have moved, but if your stance is off 20 degrees, the target won't be where you can hit it!). Is the string comfortable in your fingers? If anything, *anything*, doesn't feel right, let down and start over. If you think something is not right and you continue anyway, you can chalk the miss up to a mental error and not a physical one. Your body told you something wasn't right; you just chose to ignore it.

Drawing the Bow

This is exactly what it sounds like, and you can practice this step on its own. Some like to practice drawing with a bow slightly to considerably heavier in draw than the bow they will shoot. This builds muscle mass and makes your regular bow feel *easy* to draw. Be sure to keep the drawing elbow up during the draw, meaning near eye level.

Anchoring

Some people don't like the term *anchoring* because it implies a complete lack of motion. These are people who apparently haven't been on a boat because anchors are anything but unmoving. For recurve shooters the draw, once started, must continue without stopping because if you stop, you may not get started again. Certainly, if you stop and then manage to restart the draw, muscle tension will occur, making the release less than smooth. The anchor requires that your drawing hand be against your chin or face, but it doesn't imply that you are stopping your draw. If this is a problem, check out the Formaster® (Formasters are available online at www.spin-wing.com). This is a form tool as well as an exercise tool that will tell you whether your draw is continuous.

Aiming

Aiming is done in any number of different ways, but whichever way you aim, it must be the same each time and must involve your total focus at this *point* in the sequence. Your vision may be on the sight aperture or on the target, but your focus, for a short time, must be on aiming. Some archers spend quite a bit of time aiming; others, seemingly little. If you are focused on anything else, your shot will happen without any aim even though that was what was supposed to happen at this point. A number of top compound shooters spend a lot of their practice time just aiming. They draw up close to a blank bale and focus on making sure everything is correct and that they are relaxed by checking one muscle at a time if necessary. Compound shooters have a lot of time at full draw that recurve shooters don't. Recurve shooters used to take a great deal of time at full draw (15 to 20 seconds despite the greater weight in hand!), but it was found to be counterproductive. The female Korean Olympic style archers have probably the most consistent form of any national team (and the most success). They spend no more than one to two seconds from full draw to the release.

Release

The release is probably the hardest part of developing excellent shots. The key is to do absolutely nothing. With 30 to 40 pounds of pressure on your string fingers it is hard to realize that all you have to do is stop holding the string. You don't have to do anything. The string will push your fingers out of the way; you don't have to move them. If your fingers relax fast enough, they will flick out of the way and the string will look like it passes right through your fingers!

Follow Through

The follow-through is what happens when you release, or loose, the string. It is not something you do; it is something that happens to you. You follow through the shot. Generally, the bow should move straight forward as a result of the recoil from the shot, and then it will roll forward more or less slowly depending on the balance of your bow. At the same time your string hand should move backward (assuming a "live release") several inches, again as a result of the recoil.

For Compound Fingers Shooters Only

Common wisdom in archery has held that shooting with a *dead release* is probably beyond 99 percent of all archers. Only a few archers had ever been able to succeed with a dead release. This has changed. (At least Steve thinks so!) In a dead release, when the string goes, the string hand remains in place on your face and does not fly back as with a "live release." Almost no one shoots a dead release with a recurve bow, at least not well enough to be competitive. But with compound bows a dead release is now a viable option. The reasoning is that with 60 to 75 percent letoff, the holding weight is such that a dead release can be held without loss of back tension. A dead release has the advantage of a very firm anchor, free of the inconsistencies of the live release (plucking). The only drawback is the potential loss of back tension as the draw is stopped before loosing the arrow (see figure 4.2, *a* and *b*).

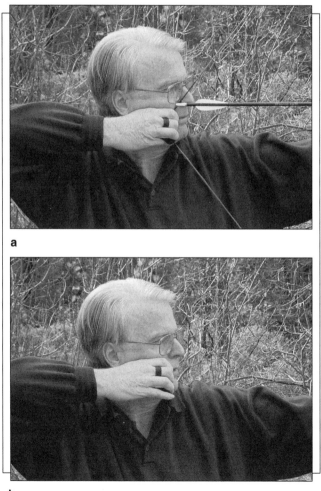

a

b

Figure 4.2 From just before the release of the string *(a)* to just after the release *(b)*, the draw hand stays in place giving a "dead" release

A great many of you have been taught that your string hand should come back to touch your shoulder. It will not do so naturally, so you must move it there yourself and is therefore not part of the true follow-through. So many people have been taught this that we see shooters at tournaments following through normally and then after some hesitation their string hands swoop through the air to land on their shoulders. Artistic as this may appear, it has no effect on the shot. We have studied videotapes of the Korean women's follow-throughs, and their hands basically never left their faces. Your shot needs to be powered by muscles in the middle of your back, and those muscles can only be squeezed so close together. Try standing in basic T form (straight up with your arms straight out to the side). Bend your elbows so that your fingertips touch your lips. Now squeeze your shoulder blades together to see how far your fingertips will move. It isn't much.

Touching your shoulder doesn't have to be a completely useless exercise. Sometimes your subconscious mind loses focus, and your conscious mind interjects with . . . *anticipation*. If you anticipate loosing the string, or following through, you will consciously change something, which will result in one different shot after another, not a good thing when you are striving to execute the same shot over and over. If you anticipate anything, it should be something that has nothing to do with the shot, such as touching your shoulder with your string hand or the bow rolling forward. These are called *completion points*. If you mess up a completion exercise (e.g., you neglect to touch your shoulder in the same place), it will have no effect on the shot because the shot was over several seconds earlier. Other than as a mechanism for dealing with anticipation in your shot, completion exercises have no real value.

Building Subconscious Execution

This may seem contradictory, but basically if you want to perform shot after shot without thinking about it, you have to think really, really hard. This happens only in practice (or dire emergencies), though. Rick McKinney, when in his heyday, winning world championships and Olympic medals, often shot 400 arrows a day (not an unusual number for an elite archer), but each shot required his full attention. He couldn't watch TV while shooting and expect it to do any good. Shots that were made while his mind wandered were of no use.

In essence, you need to tell yourself, *That was a good shot, That release was sloppy,* or *That follow-through was perfect.* You are training your brain. You want to focus on the good and eliminate the bad parts of your shot, and you need to do it piece by piece. You can't practice two things at one time. Recently Steve had some tension popping up in his bow hand several seconds into his shot. In practice, he stood in front of a blank bale, drew to anchor and focused on keeping his bow hand relaxed; then he let down. Over and over. Then, with the same focus on relaxing his bow hand, he moved on to executing shots. He was retraining his mind not to flex the muscles in his bow hand during a shot. Why did the hand get tense? Darned if we know; it just did. It doesn't now, though.

You can only think about one thing at a time, so what should you think about? The only answer is the feel of the shot up to and including the predraw. From then on you will be thinking about aiming. Some archers use key words to help them focus, such as *relax* or *follow through* or *aim (aim, aim . . .)*. Some archers think of their key words during the shot; others think of them in preparation for a shot. Some teachers will tell you to concentrate on the feel of the shot all the way through because aiming only distorts your perceptions. You will have to find out what really works for you here.

If you go to the practice range and, as we say, fling some arrows, you can have an enjoyable session, but not a useful one. You must think about what is happening in one piece of your sequence, and maybe only one per practice session, if you want to excel.

Troubleshooting

What happens when the wheels come off and you can't seem to shoot well at all? If it is a practice day, quitting is a good option. You never want to practice making bad shots. If it's the last couple of arrows on the first day of a two-day shoot, you have to try to recover your good form and execution before the next day. Unfortunately, all of our normal reactions to trouble (worry, anxiety, anticipation of failure) exacerbate the problem. Take a short break and refresh yourself. Then take out your shot sequence list and methodically work your way down the list to see if it is a form breakdown or a mental breakdown. Form breakdowns can come from something as seemingly trivial as having sweaty palms due to hot weather, which is causing your bow hand to slide around into slightly different positions.

Someone we know (and who will remain nameless) started chewing a stick of gum to relax and shot three high shots before figuring out that gum between your teeth lowers your jaw and your anchor point! If the cause is physical and you have established a habit of practicing, as Claudia says over and over, just one thing at a time, you can probably work out a simple solution in short order. You can then go to bed confident that you have dealt with your problem and will shoot well the next day.

If the problem is mental, you probably won't be able to deal with it on the practice range, but you might. Rick McKinney tells the story of practicing before a big competition. His coach came around to ask how he was doing. Rick proceeded to tell him how poorly he was shooting and shared a litany of problems he was experiencing. His coach stopped him, pointed to his shooting towel, and asked, "Is that a crying towel?" It was not an unsubtle hint that he needed to settle down and execute shots like the champion he was, which he subsequently did. Coaches can offer invaluable insight into what is going on for you at the moment, if they *know* you. If they are just walking by, don't expect miracles.

Building a Shot Sequence (Compound Shooters)

The shot sequence for compound bow archers differs in a few places. I won't repeat any of the steps that are the same as for recurve shooters, so refer to the preceding if you skipped over it. Here is Steve's shot sequence, as an example. Your sequence may be longer or shorter. If you shoot with fingers rather than a release, for example, the sequence would be different.

1. Take your stance
2. Nock an arrow
3. Hook up the release
4. Set your hands
5. Predraw
6. Draw the bow
7. Anchor
8. Check the bubble
9. Check the peep
10. Check (go or no go)
11. Aim (aim, aim!)
12. Release (a surprise!)
13. Follow through

Hooking Up the Release

If you shoot with a release, you need to hook it up on the bowstring. There are many different types of releases. Most target shooters shoot a handheld release, but some of the world's top archers do shoot wrist strap releases. Steve uses a thumb-actuated release. Others have success with little finger-actuated releases, triggerless releases (the so-called back tension releases), and letoff releases (you start with the trigger pulled and slowly relax it). The kind you shoot is generally a matter of personal preference. We know of no studies that prove one type of release to be better than another.

Steve's release is a rope release. Some prefer to use a D loop to hook up to. Some releases attach directly to the bowstring. Each has advantages and disadvantages. We generally don't recommend a direct-to-bowstring release (such as caliper releases) because of the wear they cause on the serving. (A broken serving during a tournament is not fun.) If you want to use a caliper release, use a D loop.

Checking the Bubble

When you get to anchor, you need to check the bubble level (if one is allowed) to see that the bow is plumb. After this point you generally do not look at the bubble again. It is only about four to seven seconds until the release goes off, and you usually don't drift off plumb in that short amount of time.

Checking the Peep

The circular body of the scope should be visible through the peep, and they should appear to be concentric (see figure 4.3). If they are not, you have the equivalent of a rifle in which the rear and front sights are not aligned, and you can't be sure where the shot is going. You can adjust either the peep hole diameter or the extension of the sight to get these to coincide.

Figure 4.3 You must be able to see the body of your telescopic sight through your peep sight to be sure they (and your eye) are aligned.

Checking (Go or No Go)

At this point either everything *feels* right or it doesn't. If anything (anything at all!) doesn't feel right, let down. This is where pros have a distinct advantage over amateurs. Amateur archers will shoot when things are "close enough." Top pros know that "close enough" isn't. If everything is right, the use of back tension completes the shot in the next several seconds.

The ideal release is one that is executed without thought—that is, subconsciously. This is generally called a surprise release. Your shot sequence must be practiced over and over again until it becomes learned. The hard part for release shooters is executing the release aid.

Whatever kind of release aid you use, you want it to go off with virtually no motion that will dislodge the bowstring from its carefully aimed position. The advantage of the compound bow is the ability to hold at full draw for considerable time and aim (aim, aim, aim). The advantage of the release aid is to get a clean loose of the string. If you move your hand or the release at the loosing of the string, you will be inconsistent. So it is best that the release operator—you—not know when the release is to go off. Just focus on being as steady as possible.

Deliberately actuating a release's trigger is called "punching the release" no matter how little movement is involved. Some archers have achieved great success as "punchers"; odds are, though, you aren't one of those. Very few shooters have the mental capacity to succeed while punching their release aids. The trap is that your conscious mind will know when the release is about to go off and anticipate what is going to happen. If you have ever flinched during a shot, you have experienced this firsthand. Your body is reacting to the shot when the shot hasn't yet occurred! This is your conscious brain's job—to anticipate what is happening so you can be prepared—so don't blame it!

For the vast majority of us, punching is not an option if you want to shoot high scores. What to do? Well, it is not complicated, but also not easy. You have to give up control. One of the easiest ways to do this is to switch to a triggerless release aid, such as a Stanislawski release. It's hard to punch a trigger that isn't there. But actually, any quality release aid can be executed without punching. Whether you use a wrist strap release or a handheld release, it is best to have significant trigger pressure with a minimum (or no) "throw" (i.e., movement of the trigger to cause release). Steve's release (a Carter "Target 3") went off at one and a quarter pounds of pressure before he sent it back to Carter for respringing. It now goes off at about 11 pounds of pressure with no noticeable movement of the trigger. That may be a bit much for you. What you want to avoid is the "hair trigger syndrome." We have seen archers sit around arguing about who had the "faster" release aid (that is, the hairiest hair trigger). We have seen these releases shot well by a few, but more often they result in arrows in the trees because they have the nasty habit of going off when you don't want them to. A reasonable guide is that you should be able to place your finger or thumb on the trigger without having to worry that it is going to go off. If you can't, the trigger is set too fast.

The next step, once you reach anchor, is to place the trigger where you can set it off without using a twitchy part of your anatomy. For wrist strap releases, the trigger should be nestled into the first joint of the finger, not on the pad (see figure 4.4). For thumb releases, the trigger should be tucked behind the first joint of the thumb, not on the pad (see figure 4.5). Then the release is triggered as you pull at full draw (because your hand elongates as you stretch it by pulling on the release aid—that is, if you are relaxed enough). This is hard to learn on your own and is well worth acquiring a coach for a couple of lessons to get a good start at it.

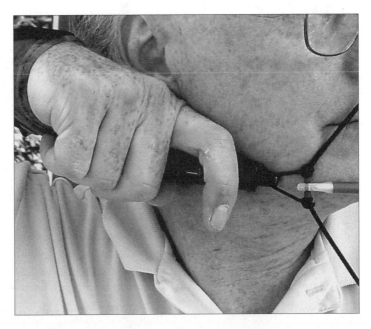

Figure 4.4 For a wrist strap release the trigger needs to be back in, or behind, the first joint of the actuating finger.

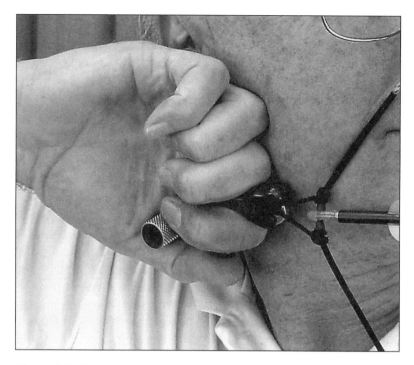

Figure 4.5   For thumb releases the trigger needs to be tucked back on the thumb, not on the pad.

Getting Off the String

Most people think that a finger tab is simply a device to protect your fingers from the pressure of the bowstring. It is that, but it also smoothes out the fleshy pads of your fingers to give you a smoother release. (We guess you could soak your fingers in leather tanning solutions to get a similar effect, but it would wreak havoc with your manicure.) There are basically two kinds of releases when you shoot "fingers": the "dead release" and, for want of a better term, the "live release."

If you shoot a recurve or longbow, the only option is a "live release." No serious Olympic style archer shoots with a dead release. The live release involves continuous motion of the drawing hand. The drawing hand begins rapidly, slows at anchor, and then jumps backward a few inches when the string leaves. At no time does it stop moving backward. To acquire a "live release," start in front of a blank bale and practice releasing the string at about half draw. Focus on relaxing the fingers of the drawing hand rather than doing something with them. Do not try to move your fingers out of the way. Remember, let the string go; don't let go of the string! The string will pull itself out of your fingers, flicking them out of the way. If you have never felt this before, hang a paint can or small pail with a few rocks in it by its bail at your side. Just stop holding the pail at some point and it will drop to the ground. You can be perfectly relaxed through the whole exercise; when you decide to stop holding the pail, it will leave your hand on its own accord. You do not have to move your fingers to release the pail.

Next, practice releasing when your draw hand just touches your face. Again, focus on relaxing your fingers to loose the arrow. If you are using a clicker, it comes next. There is no substitute we know of for repetition here, but you don't need targets; you do need to focus on what you are doing. Don't try to get off a hundred practice shots while listening to a ball game!

In a dead release, the drawing hand stops at anchor and stays fixed when the string leaves (see figure 4.2, *a* and *b*, on page 50). A dead release is considered by virtually everyone to be a form flaw for recurve and longbow shooters. Some say that a dead release is a form flaw for all archers, but we think that the compound bow makes such a release more than feasible. The key is that the compound bow's letoff leaves only 15 to 20 pounds at most *in hand* at anchor. With proper back action, creeping and collapsing won't happen, and the shot can be loosed cleanly with the hand anchored on the face. Since your hand never leaves your face, you can't pluck the bowstring or execute any number of other flawed releases that plague archers who must shoot a live release. When Steve returned to finger shooting after six years behind a release, he studied all of the champion com-pound finger shooters he could observe directly, and they all shot with a dead release. In any case, whichever style of finger release you choose, it will require quite a bit of practice to perfect.

Using a Clicker

The clicker was invented as a "draw check"; that is, it told you when you had pulled the arrow back far enough. An arrow pulled half an inch past average is going to fly far higher than one pulled half an inch less than average. Developing a consistent draw with a recurve bow requires huge amounts of practice, even with a clicker telling you when you are at full draw. A clicker is just a springlike device that generally slides along the arrow, then falls off the point as it is pulled past, making a click (see figure 4.6). It started out as a draw check, but is far more than that today. All Olympic-style shooters use a clicker, so if you want to be competitive, you will too. Some traditional styles of archery forbid them or limit their use or shape. If you

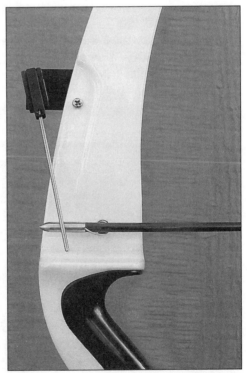

Figure 4.6 A clicker slides down the arrow shaft as the arrow is drawn, eventually falling off and making a click sound or feel. This tells you that you have drawn the bow the exact length you set and that the shot can be loosed.

are allowed one, you really ought to try shooting with one. They are generally considered unnecessary for shooting compound bows, but many do use them. Frank and Becky Pearson, top pros for decades, even shot compound bows with clickers using release aids!

Not only do clickers serve as draw checks, but they also "trigger" the shot. When you shoot a bow and arrow with your fingers on the string, you will know when the shot is going to be loosed because you have to consciously relax your fingers to do so. This can lead to anticipating the shot, which can lead to flinched shots, plucked shots, and so on.

When the clicker was first introduced, it was inserted into the shot sequence as one more thing to check. The shot didn't go off for seconds after the clicker informed the archer she was at full draw. Now shots are loosed immediately after the clicker clicks. Do not misunderstand. It is not really a trigger of the shot; it is merely a signal to shoot. When you shoot with a clicker, you have to have the shot entirely in order when the clicker goes off, but you are still in control. Good clicker shooters will let down if the clicker goes off during the draw but the rest of the shot isn't together yet. (This can happen, for example, when the adrenaline gets pumping and you draw a bit too strongly.) The clicker does set the tempo for the shot, though, and does give you a hard-to-predict signal that the shot is ready to go. Thus, it adds an element of surprise to the loose much like a release aid does. In the 1970s there was a vocal debate over whether to use a clicker on recurve bows. That debate has been settled, and the clicker won. If you are allowed to use one, try it.

Placing Your Focus

There is some debate on where you should place your focus while aiming. Some say you should focus on the target; others say you should focus on the sight aperture or scope. We agree. Focusing anywhere else is silly. Try both and see which works best for you. To give it a fair try, you must execute a fair number of shots with your aiming eye focused on the target and with the aperture "fuzzy." Then do the reverse—focus on the aperture with the target fuzzy. As a compound-release shooter, Steve focuses on the aperture because there is so much to check (bubble, peep concentricity), but then switches to the target. So, you can even do both. Check to see which is more comfortable and which makes for better scores.

Listen to Your Equipment

Because we are not perfect, we all tend to have better days and poorer days. This is no surprise. What may be a surprise is that your equipment may help you in the struggle to shoot well even on what may be one of your poorer days. You need to learn to listen to your equipment.

Listening to your equipment sometimes involves your ears and sometimes does not. Steve says his compound makes a particular "thrummm" sound when he gets a clean finger release on his shot. When he is struggling with his release, he will focus on just trying to reproduce that sound, and his release will get cleaner. Sometimes listening to your equipment involves your mind. If you shoot a nice group of arrows on a target but the group is too low to score well, is it because the bow is defective? Probably not, but it is a possibility.

Generally, we consider good groups to be a sign of consistent shooting. Low groups can come from a mis-set sight, dropping your bow arm because of fatigue, a broken serving causing your nocking point to elevate, a loose aperture or scope, or half a dozen form flaws (such as a misplaced anchor point). You are getting a sign that something is not right, but what? Here you have to realize that you are not going to hear your bow say, "I have a loose serving, stupid!", but it is definitely saying something. First we would run through the list checking everything we could that was easy to check. Is my scope loose? Did I mis-set my sight? Has my nocking point indicator slipped? (You do carry a bow square in your quiver, don't you?) If we find no obvious mechanical defect, we replay the shots in memory trying to detect fatigue or lapses in shot sequence.

Here's where Frank Pearson's recommendation that you keep your shot sequence written down on a card in your quiver comes in. You can run down it quickly without having to tax your memory. (You are not supposed to be thinking of it during competition, remember!) If we can only come up with a guess as to what it was, we then go for corrective action. If we think the problem has been a dropping bow arm, we execute the next few shots after telling ourselves *strong bow arm* or any other key words of the same effect. Steve was struggling so much during the first day of a FITA shoot that he used the key words *strong bow arm* and *finish the shot* on each shot during the second day and finished the day with a personal best score. Generally our equipment tells us everything we need to know if we can just learn to listen to it.

Executing Under Duress

All of the previous discussion assumes perfect conditions for shooting. What happens when the conditions are less than perfect? In chapter 10 we will discuss the measures you can take to deal with shooting in wind, rain, and heat and humidity. Here we will just consider the effects of terrain on executing strong shots.

Shooting Uphill and Downhill

Target archery is on the flat, but field archery can consist of quite a few uphill and downhill shots. Much has been written about this subject, but remember two aspects. One is that you must maintain *upper-body form*. You should try to bend at the waist and adjust to the slope or uneven footing below the waist. Maintaining upper-body geometry is the best measure of success in shooting up-, down-, and sidehill shots.

The second aspect regards shooting up and down slopes. These shots always seem to be *shorter* than they are marked. Yes, shorter for both kinds of shots! Figure 4.7 will get you the approximate yardage to set your sight. Computer programs such as *Archer's Advantage* (www.archersadvantage.com) will do an even better job. You still have to practice these shots, though. The computer won't do it for you.

FIGURE 4.7   SIGHT DISTANCE CHART

Find or estimate the angle plus or minus 2 or 3 degrees, then slide down the left-hand column to that number. Slide across to the column closest to the yardage of the target for the correct distance to set your sight. For example, a 20-degree uphill or downhill shot marked for 45 yards/meters should be shot at 42.3 meters (or a "cut" of 2.7 yards/meters). If the marked yardage is not 45, but 44, take the 2.7 yards/meters from 44 to get 41.3 yards/meters.

0	20	25	30	35	40	45	50	55	60	65	70	75	80	85	90	95	100
5	19.9	24.9	29.9	34.9	39.8	44.8	49.8	54.8	59.8	64.8	69.7	74.7	79.7	84.7	89.7	94.6	99.6
10	19.7	24.6	29.5	34.5	39.4	44.3	49.2	54.2	59.1	64.0	68.9	73.9	78.8	83.7	88.6	93.6	98.5
15	19.3	24.1	29.0	33.8	38.6	43.5	48.3	53.1	58.0	62.8	67.6	72.4	77.3	82.1	86.9	91.8	96.6
20	18.8	23.5	28.2	32.9	37.6	42.3	47.0	51.7	56.4	61.1	65.8	70.5	75.2	79.9	84.6	89.3	94.0
25	18.1	22.7	27.2	31.7	36.3	40.8	45.3	49.8	54.4	58.9	63.4	68.0	72.5	77.0	81.6	86.1	90.6
30	17.3	21.7	26.0	30.3	34.6	39.0	43.3	47.6	52.0	56.3	60.6	65.0	69.3	73.6	77.9	82.3	86.6
35	16.4	20.5	24.6	28.7	32.8	36.9	41.0	45.1	49.1	53.2	57.3	61.4	65.5	69.6	73.7	77.8	81.9
40	15.3	19.2	23.0	26.8	30.6	34.5	38.3	42.1	46.0	49.8	53.6	57.5	61.3	65.1	68.9	72.8	76.6
45	14.1	17.7	21.2	24.7	28.3	31.8	35.4	38.9	42.4	46.0	49.5	53.0	56.6	60.1	63.6	67.2	70.7

Shooting at Elevation

If you get sight marks at sea level and then go to a shoot at 5,000 feet elevation (or vice versa), don't count on your sight markings being the same. We don't know if it is the difference in air density or what, but if you are expecting to have a large change in elevation, get there early enough to check all of your sight markings. Also be aware that large elevation changes have an effect on you physically and may cause you to feel out of breath and lightheaded or even lethargic. If the competition is really important, see if you can get there a couple of days early to acclimate.

Wrapping Up

So, is archery really as simple as "pull back and let go"? We said the answer is yes and no. The no part comes when you are struggling to advance past the stage of being a beginner. Then it gets complicated as you struggle to create a regular, consistent shot sequence. When you have shot hundreds, even thousands, of shots, executing them becomes more mental, more of a feeling than a series of physical steps. Then it gets easy again.

But don't worry. If you decide that you want to compete at an elite level, it gets hard again. (We wouldn't want to disappoint you "If it weren't hard, it wouldn't be worth doing" types!)

5

Achieving a Physical Edge

Annette M. Musta

Archers often spend large amounts of money upgrading their equipment. They will try every new gadget, learn every new technique, and listen to every coach in an effort to increase their scores and improve their shooting. Archers do all of this while ignoring the most important element of their shot, the engine that runs it all—their body.

Like any engine, the human body requires fuel for activity. The fuel for body function is adenosine triphosphate, or ATP. The body stores a small amount of ATP, enough for only a couple of seconds of muscular work. Most of the ATP necessary for muscle contraction is produced on demand through one of four metabolic pathways. Archery is an endurance sport. It requires a constant expenditure of energy over a long period. The metabolic pathways for endurance activities are aerobic glycolysis and fatty acid oxidation. Both of these systems require oxygen.

Aerobic synthesis of ATP occurs within the mitochondria of the cells. The mitochondria are the "power plants" of the cell. Their ability to produce ATP is only limited by the ability of the cardiorespiratory system to deliver oxygen to the cells. There are differences in the two systems. Aerobic glycolysis uses the body's glycogen stores. Fatty acid oxidation uses the fatty acid stores in the body. Both aerobic energy pathways require large amounts of oxygen. The body depends on the aerobic pathways for lower-intensity endurance activities such as archery.

As with all fitness information, you should first consult your doctor for clearance before performing any physical fitness program or training.

Cardiorespiratory Conditioning

The cardiovascular system is responsible for transporting oxygen to the tissues and cells and removing wastes from the body. The respiratory system oxygenates and removes carbon dioxide from the body and helps to regulate the acid–base balance of the body. The external respiratory system is responsible for the exchange of oxygen and carbon dioxide between the environment and the lungs. Internal respiration takes place at the cellular level. Cellular oxygenation is an integral part of the aerobic production of ATP.

Cardiorespiratory conditioning improves the efficiency of the blood transport system. The increased demands on the cardiorespiratory system during cardio training improves the oxygen-carrying capacity of the blood and increases the amount of hemoglobin, the stroke volume, and the ability of the cells to use oxygen for ATP production.

An efficient blood transport system allows a longer duration of low-intensity activity. Fit archers have a distinct advantage over their competitors. Fit archers have longer endurance and recover from a grueling day of shooting faster than unfit archers. Fit archers have greater muscle endurance, enabling them to maintain the form of their shot throughout the competition.

Cardio conditioning will lower the resting heart rate and the recovery heart rate. The resting heart rate is the number of times the heart beats per minute while at rest. This is a measurement of the overall cardiorespiratory conditioning. The lower resting heart rate of fit archers makes them less susceptible to the rush of nervous adrenaline during high-tension shooting situations, reducing the effects of the racing heart, sweaty palms, and panic breathing common to this condition. An added benefit of weight-bearing aerobic exercise is that it strengthens the bones, providing a good skeletal base for the archery shot.

Cardiorespiratory conditioning consists of any activity that consistently increases the heart rate. Walking, bicycling, running, rowing, aerobic dance, kick boxing, hiking, trail running, and swimming are a few examples. This is the exercise *mode*. The *duration* is measured as the amount of time spent at the target heart rate. *Intensity* is measured by the heart rate. To be effective, the workout should be performed in the target heart rate zone for the desired duration. Less intense workouts have to be performed more frequently and for longer periods to achieve the same results as more intense workouts. The *frequency* is the number of times the cardio workout is performed in a given week.

- **Frequency.** Use the following guidelines to determine your frequency of exercise based on your score on the cardiovascular conditioning test. See "Measuring Your Current Level of Cardiovascular Fitness" on page 66 to assess your current level of cardiovascular fitness.

Score	Frequency of exercise sessions	Rest period between sessions
Poor or fair	2-3 times per week	36-48 hours
Good	3-4 times per week	24 hours
Excellent	5-6 times per week	24 hours

- **Duration.** Duration is the number of minutes spent at target training levels per exercise session. The duration depends on the mode and intensity. More intense exercise cannot, and should not, be sustained for extended periods unless you are in the excellent category and have proper training and supervision. The higher the intensity level of the activity, the shorter the duration necessary for comparable results. Use the following general guidelines for duration.

Category	Duration of Exercise Sessions
Poor	5-10 minutes per session
Fair	10-15 minutes per session
Good	15-45 minutes per session
Excellent	30-60 minutes per session

As your cardiovascular conditioning improves, you should increase the duration of your exercise sessions. After the first four to eight weeks, increase your duration five minutes per week as tolerated. Unless you are involved in a low-intensity activity, you should not exceed 60 minutes in duration.

- **Intensity.** Intensity is the exercise workload. Intensity is commonly referred to as your *target heart rate*. You should aim to keep the intensity of your workout in this zone. Your target heart rate is a percentage of your maximal heart rate. Use the following age-based formula to calculate your target heart rate (get out your calculators, this requires decimals!).

Target Heart Rate Zone Calculation
Maximal heart rate = 220 − your age
Target heart rate (minimal) = maximal heart rate × 0.50
Target heart rate (maximal) = maximal heart rate ×0.75

Measuring Your Current Level of Cardiovascular Fitness

Equipment Needed: a 12-inch step and a stopwatch

Procedure: Step briskly up and down on the 12-inch step using the following cycle: right foot up, left foot up, right foot down, left foot down. Try to maintain a pace of 24 cycles per minute. Time yourself for three minutes using the stopwatch. At the end of three minutes, sit down and find your pulse (two fingers on the outside of the neck or wrist). After one minute of rest, find your heart rate by counting your pulse for 15 seconds and multiplying by 4 to get beats per minute. This is your "recovery heart rate." Compare your results with the following chart. Record your level of cardiovascular fitness. Repeat this test every three months to monitor your progress.

Age (years)	18-25		26-35		36-45		46-55		56-65	
	M	F	M	F	M	F	M	F	M	F
Excellent	<89	<98	<89	<99	<96	<102	<97	<104	<97	<104
Good	90-105	99-117	90-107	100-119	97-112	103-118	98-116	105-120	98-112	105-118
Fair	106-128	118-140	108-128	120-138	113-130	119-140	117-132	121-135	113-129	119-139
Poor	>128	>140	>128	>138	>130	>140	>132	>135	>129	>139

Reprinted from Personal Trainer's Handbook, ACE, 1999.

You must learn how to accurately measure your heart rate to keep your workouts in a safe category. The easiest way is to take your pulse, either on the side of the neck or at the wrist. (Warning! Do not press hard on the side of your neck. This is the carotid pulse and you have sense receptors that will change your pulse if you press too hard.) Another way is to purchase an electronic heart rate monitor. They are available at sporting goods stores in many different price ranges.

You should keep your heart rate (pulse) in your target zone for the duration of your fitness session. Individuals in the poor or fair category should aim for the minimal target heart rate. Individuals in the good or excellent category should aim for the maximal number. Increases in target heart rate should be done in small increments over six to eight weeks of training and should not exceed the maximal target heart rate unless you are under supervision.

It is important to warm up and cool down when you exercise. The warm-up should consist of 5 to 10 minutes of light movement (e.g., walking). Cool-down should include 5 to 10 minutes of light movement combined with stretching of all muscle groups.

Figure 5.1 lists simple cardio programs for athletes at all fitness levels. The well-trained athlete can further increase the benefits of cardio training by using interval training, and any cardio program can be adapted to include an interval program. Interval training at the intensity in the program shown in table 5.1 is designed only for well-conditioned athletes. Athletes who score in the excellent category can include interval training in their program.

FIGURE 5.1   SAMPLE CARDIO PROGRAMS

Cardio Beginners (Poor/Fair)

Frequency
2-3 days/week

Rest period
24-48 hours

Duration
10-15 minutes/session

Intensity
Minimal target heart rate

Mode
Walking, light aerobics, bicycling, swimming

Schedule
- Monday - Walk for 15 minutes
- Wednesday - Swim for 15 minutes
- Friday - Cardio exercise tape

Cardio Intermediates (Good)

Frequency
3-4 days each week

Rest period
24 hours

Duration
15-45 minutes each session

Intensity
Median target heart rate

Mode
Bicycling, swimming, rowing, in-line skating, jogging

Schedule
- Monday and Tuesday - Jog for 35 minutes
- Friday - Swim for 40 minutes
- Saturday - Bicycle for 45 minutes

Cardio Advanced (Excellent)

Frequency
4-6 days each week

Rest period
24 hours

Duration
45-60 minutes each session

Intensity
Maximal target heart rate

Mode
Bicycling, swimming, running/jogging, in-line skating, rowing

Schedule
- Monday - Swim for 30 minutes, jog for 30 minutes
- Tuesday - Bicycle for 60 minutes
- Wednesday - 60-minute aerobics class
- Thursday - Swim for 20 minutes, bicycle for 20 minutes, jog for 20 minutes
- Saturday - Bicycle for 2 hours

Interval training consists of very high intensity cycles of exercise within the cardio program and maximizes the body's use of oxygen and the production of ATP. The interval cycle contains a period of high-intensity exercise at 70 to 85 percent of the maximal heart rate followed by a rest period at the median heart rate of 65 percent of maximal heart rate. The cycle is repeated for the duration of the exercise period. The program shown in table 5.1 starts with a comprehensive warm-up that gradually raises the heart rate, followed by a complete stretching routine. The high intensity of interval training causes a muscle overload that can increase the risk for injury, so the warm-up phase is necessary. You'll need a heart rate monitor for interval training. After completing the program, stretch each major muscle group of the entire body.

TABLE 5.1   INTERVAL TRAINING

	Speed (mph)	% of max. heart rate (min.)	Time
Warm-up	2.0-2.5	50-60%	5
Warm-up	3.0-3.5	50-60%	5 *
Interval	4.5-5.5 (fast jog)	65-75%	5
Recovery	3.5-4.0	60-65 %	3
Interval	4.5-5.5	75-80%	5
Recovery	3.5-4.0	60-65%	3
Interval (high intensity)	5.5-6.5 (fast run)	85-90 %	2
Recovery	3.5-4.0	60-65 %	3
High intensity	5.5-6.5	85-90%	2
Cool-down	3.0-3.5	60-65 %	4
Cool-down	2.0-2.5	50-60 %	5

*After warm-up, step off the treadmill and stretch the calves, hamstrings, and quadriceps.

Individual program design can be accomplished by adapting the treadmill program as a guide. Remember, though, that programs should be adapted for each individual by a certified trainer. Use the heart rates and time intervals from table 5.1 to adapt your program to surface walking or running programs or bicycling, swimming, in-line skating, rowing, or any other mode of cardiorespiratory exercise.

Strength Training

Archery is a sport of repetition and causes imbalance in the muscles of the body. The bow arm is pushing out at the same time as the drawing arm is pulling back. Increasing muscle strength in the upper body (arms, shoulders, and back) evens out the imbalance. It is not necessary to work each side of the body differently. A strength program is not meant to counteract the repetition of training your archery shot hundreds of times a day. The goal of the upper-body strength program for the advanced archer is to increase the conditioning of the muscles used in the archery shot.

Endurance sports use primarily slow-twitch muscle fibers. To build slow-twitch muscle fibers, each muscle and muscle group is exercised at moderate resistance and high repetitions. Moderate resistance is defined as 40 to 70 percent of your one-repetition maximum (1RM). To build 1RM, muscles are exercised for strength gain. Strength-gain training exercises the muscles at high resistance and low repetition. High resistance is defined as 80 to 90 percent of your 1RM. A comprehensive archery strength training program will work for strength gain, transition to strength endurance, and end with maintenance as the competitive season approaches. Strength-gain training will interfere with archery training, whereas strength-endurance training supplements archery training. Maintenance training is designed for use during the competitive season. If done properly, you can train to peak during the competitive season.

Archery appears to use only the muscles of the upper body. In reality, the entire body is used in the archery shot. The muscles of the legs and trunk provide a strong base for extensive standing during competitions (not to mention the miles of walking involved in a FITA competition). If your body is a machine, the legs and butt are the structural support for that machine.

The abdominal muscles and the muscles of the lower back provide stability during the draw sequence by stabilizing the counteracting forces of the upper body. They also continue the work of the lower body in providing the strong base of support for the archery draw.

The muscles of the arms, the upper back and chest, and the shoulder are all actively involved in the draw itself. Strength gain training these muscles followed by strength-endurance training will increase the ability of these muscles to maintain the correct form of the archery draw during the length of a long archery competition.

A proper strength program should include core exercises incorporating all of the major muscle groups and isolation exercises for specific muscle groups. Strength training can be designed to increase the bulk of the muscles or to tone the muscles. Training your muscles outside of your archery training will build efficient muscle tissue that you can use during your archery shot. Finally, training in any sport can lead to overuse injuries. When the body is called on to repeat an action, it can eventually break down. Joint injuries are the most common form of overuse injuries. Common injuries to archers include shoulder and back injuries. In effect, strength training is a form of cross training. It enables the archer to build strong muscles and joints using the same muscle groups in the archery shot but in a different way. The change in demand on the muscles can counteract overuse injuries.

Strength Training Programs

An archery strength training program is divided into three areas: upper body, core and lower body, and rotator cuff muscles. The muscles of the upper body include the major shoulder muscles (deltoids), the major upper back muscles (latissimus dorsi, trapezius, rhomboids), the arm muscles (biceps and triceps), and the chest muscles. The core muscles include the muscles of the abdomen and the lower back. The lower body muscles are the gluteus, the quadriceps, and the calf muscles. The rotator cuff muscles are discussed later. The strength training program is divided into three phases: strength gain, strength endurance, and strength maintenance.

Strength Gain

The strength gain program works the major muscle groups of the body. This part of the program should be performed no more than three times a week with a minimum 24-hour rest period between sessions. The strength gain program should be scheduled at the start of the off-season and should be performed after archery practice for the day. The gain cycle runs for four weeks with a two-week maintenance period for a six-week cycle. The cycle can be repeated for a maximum of three gain/recovery cycles or until the competition schedule deems it appropriate to switch to an endurance cycle. The strength gain cycle improves the performance of fast-twitch muscle fibers and increases the 1RM of the muscles. *Always use a spotter when working with heavy weights.*

Gain Cycle One (Four Weeks)

Exercises

Squats, stationary lunges, modified deadlifts, calf raises, upright rows, bench presses, pullovers, bent-over rows, military presses, preacher curls, and triceps curls

Day	Weight as % of 1RM	Repetitions/sets
Monday	75-80%	6-8/3
Wednesday	75-80%	6-8/3
Friday	75-80%	6-8/3

Stabilizer Exercises

Bow, crunches, oblique crunches: 10 repetitions/three sets

Recovery Cycle (Four Weeks)

Exercises

- Squats, alternating lunges, hamstring curls, push-ups, sit-ups, triceps dips: no weights

  Repetitions: 15 reps each side; *frequency:* three times a week

- Light weights (3-5 pounds): biceps curls, military presses

  Repetitions: 15 reps each side; *frequency:* three times a week

- Seated row with resistance band

  Repetitions: 15 reps each side; *frequency:* three times a week

Gain Cycle Two (Four Weeks)

Exercises

Squats, stationary lunges, modified deadlifts, calf raises, upright rows, bench presses, pullovers, bent-over rows, military presses, preacher curls, and triceps curls

Day	Weight as % of 1RM	Repetitions/sets
Monday	80-85%	4-6/3
Wednesday	80-85%	4-6/3
Friday	80-85%	4-6/3

Stabilizer Exercises

Bow, crunches, oblique crunches: 10 repetitions/three sets

Recovery Cycle (Two Weeks)

Exercises

- Squats, alternating lunges, hamstring curls, push-ups, sit-ups, triceps dips: no weights

  Repetitions: 15 reps each side; *frequency:* three times a week

- Light weights (3-5 pounds): biceps curls, military presses

  Repetitions: 15 reps each side; *frequency:* three times a week

- Seated row with resistance band

  Repetitions: 15 reps each side; *frequency:* three times a week

Gain Cycle Three (Two Weeks)

Exercises

Squats, stationary lunges, modified deadlifts, calf raises, upright rows, bench presses, pullovers, bent-over rows, military presses, preacher curls, and triceps curls

Day	Weight as % of 1RM	Repetitions/sets
Monday	85-90%	4/3
Wednesday	85-90%	4/3
Friday	85-90%	4/3

Stabilizer Exercises

Bow, crunches, oblique crunches: 10 repetitions/three sets

Recovery Cycle (One Week)

Exercises

- Squats, alternating lunges, hamstring curls, push-ups, sit-ups, triceps dips: no weights

    Repetitions: 15 reps each side; *frequency:* three times a week
- Light weights (3-5 pounds): biceps curls, military presses

    Repetitions: 15 reps each side; *frequency:* three times a week
- Seated row with resistance band

    Repetitions: 15 reps each side; *frequency:* three times a week

Alternate Cycle Three (Two Weeks)

Strength can be enhanced through plyometric training, which consists of high-intensity exercises done in short bursts. You will need a 5- to 12-pound medicine ball for these exercises. Some exercises require a partner.

Squat Lift

Targeted muscles: entire body

Equipment Needed: medicine ball

Procedure: Stand with feet hip-width apart. Place the medicine ball between your feet. Perform a proper squat and grasp the ball with both hands. In one swift movement, stand up while moving the ball to above your head, keeping your arms straight. At the top of the motion, bend your arms at the elbows and lower the ball behind your head. Slowly return to the starting position. Repeat.

One-Arm Ball Bounce

Targeted muscles: back and shoulders

Equipment needed: medicine ball and a partner

Procedure: Stand about six feet from your partner with your left shoulders facing each other. Hold the ball at shoulder height in your right hand. With a strong swift downward motion, bounce the ball off the floor to your partner. Your partner repeats by bouncing the ball back to you. Perform 15 sets on the right side and then 15 sets on the left side.

Squat Jump

Targeted muscles: lower body

Procedure: Stand next to a high wall with your feet hip-width apart. Slowly lower into a squat position. In a swift motion from the squatting position, jump as high as possible. Return to the starting position and repeat.

Chest Press Toss

Targeted muscles: chest and triceps

Equipment needed: medicine ball and a partner

Procedure: Stand facing your partner approximately five feet apart. Hold the ball at chest level, arms bent, ball touching your chest. In a swift motion, throw the ball to your partner. The partner repeats the motion and throws back to you. Each partner makes 15 throws.

Strength Endurance

The strength endurance program is designed to increase your muscle endurance. Endurance exercises require slow-twitch muscle fibers. Slow-twitch muscles enable you to repeatedly draw the bow during training and competition. Muscles must be trained in a different way for endurance. The motions are slow and controlled. The exercises will increase the number of slow-twitch fibers and will improve the nerve and blood supply to the muscles. Endurance strength gains are achieved by using light weight, a resistance band, or body weight and a higher number of repetitions. The endurance program should be performed after archery practice program three to five times a week with a minimum of 24 hours between sessions. The strength endurance cycle lasts six weeks and should end a minimum of two weeks before the start of the competitive season. The cycle can be repeated. All exercises are explained in detail later in this chapter.

Strength Endurance Cycle One (Four Weeks)

Exercises

Leg curls, leg extensions, alternating lunges, triceps kickbacks, biceps curls, deltoid raises, lateral pull-downs, chest presses, calf raises, bent-over rows

Day	Weight as % of 1RM	Repetitions/sets
Monday	50-55%	10/3
Tuesday	50-55%	10/3
Thursday	50-55%	10/3
Friday	50-55%	10/3

Stabilizer Exercises

Bow, crunches, oblique crunches: 10 repetitions/two sets

Alternate Program

Use a resistance band in place of static weights one session a week.

Recovery Cycle (One Week)

Exercises

- Squats, alternating lunges, hamstring curls, push-ups, sit-ups, triceps dips: no weights
  Repetitions: 15 reps each side; *frequency:* three times a week
- Light weights (3-5 pounds): biceps curls, military presses
  Repetitions: 15 reps each side; *frequency:* three times a week
- Seated row with resistance band
  Repetitions: 15 reps each side; *frequency:* three times a week

Strength Endurance Cycle Two (Four Weeks)

Exercises

Leg curls, leg extensions, alternating lunges, triceps kickbacks, biceps curls, deltoid raises, lateral pull-downs, chest presses, calf raises, bent-over rows

Day	Weight as % of 1RM	Repetitions/sets
Monday	50-55%	15-18/3
Tuesday	50-55%	15-18/3
Thursday	50-55%	15-18/3
Friday	50-55%	15-18/3

Stabilizer Exercises

Bow, crunches, oblique crunches: 10 repetitions/two sets

Alternate Program

Use a resistance band in place of static weights one session a week.

Recovery Cycle (One Week)

Exercises

- Squats, alternating lunges, hamstring curls, push-ups, sit-ups, triceps dips: no weights
  Repetitions: 15 reps each side; *frequency:* three times a week
- Light weights (3-5 pounds): biceps curls, military presses
  Repetitions: 15 reps each side; *frequency:* three times a week
- Seated row with resistance band
  Repetitions: 15 reps each side; *frequency:* three times a week

Strength Endurance Cycle Three (Four Weeks)

Exercises

Leg curls, leg extensions, alternating lunges, triceps kickbacks, biceps curls, deltoid raises, lateral pull-downs, chest presses, calf raises, bent-over rows

Day	Weight as % of 1RM	Repetitions/sets
Monday	50-55%	20-25/3
Tuesday	50-55%	20-25/3
Thursday	50-55%	20-25/3
Friday	50-55%	20-25/3

Stabilizer Exercises

Bow, crunches, oblique crunches: 10 repetitions/two sets

Alternate Program

Use a resistance band in place of static weights one session a week.

Recovery Cycle (One Week)

Exercises

- Squats, alternating lunges, hamstring curls, push-ups, sit-ups, triceps dips: no weights

  Repetitions: 15 reps each side; *frequency:* three times a week
- Light weights (3-5 pounds): biceps curls, military presses

  Repetitions: 15 reps each side; *frequency:* three times a week
- Seated row with resistance band

  Repetitions: 15 reps each side; *frequency:* three times a week

Alternate Endurance Program

Each of these exercises requires very slow movement with long hold times. Move very slowly to get into the endurance position. Perform three reps of each exercise.

Wall Squat

Stand with your back to a wall. Slowly lower into a squat position with your back against the wall, knees bent at no more than a 90-degree angle. Hold this position for a count of 10. Slowly return to the starting position. Work up to a count of 60.

Bridge

Lie on your back, knees bent, hands flat on the ground at your sides. Slowly push your pelvis toward the ceiling. Hold for a count of 10. Slowly lower to the starting position. Work up to a count of 60.

Plank

Start in a push-up position, hands slightly wider than shoulder width. Slowly lower into the plank position balancing on your hands and feet; no other part of your body should touch the floor. Hold for a count of 10 and slowly return to the starting position. Work up to a count of 60.

Reverse Curl

Sit on the floor with your knees bent and your hands resting on your knees. Slowly lower your upper body back toward the floor, stopping at a position halfway down. Hold for a count of 10. Return to the starting position. Work up to a count of 60.

Archery Pull

This exercise requires a resistance band. Hold the loose ends of the band in your bow hand, and grasp the loop in your drawing hand using your standard archery fingering. Slowly pull back on the band to your anchor position. Hold for a count of 10. Slowly let down. Repeat 10 times. Repeat on the opposite side. Work up to a hold of 60 seconds. Once you can hold for 60 seconds, add resistance by shortening the resistance band. When adding resistance, reduce your hold to a count of 10 and work back up to a count of 60.

Maintenance Strength Program

This program is designed to maintain the strength gains made during the gain and endurance cycles. The maintenance phase occurs during the competitive season. This program should be done a maximum of twice a week. The maintenance program uses very light weights and moderate reps.

Maintenance Strength Cycle

Exercises

Squats, modified deadlifts, stationary lunges, biceps curls, triceps kickbacks, upright rows, single-arm rows, calf raises

Day	Weight as % of 1RM	Repetitions/sets
Tuesday	10-15%	8/3
Friday	10-15%	8/3

Stabilizer Exercises

Bow, crunches, oblique crunches: 10 repetitions/two sets

Weight Training Exercise Descriptions

The following list includes instructions for the basic weight training exercises used in the previously outlined programs. Each exercise fully describes the movement and lists the muscles worked and the equipment needed. Learn the movement of each exercise before adding weights. Watch yourself in a mirror or work with a certified trainer to learn the proper positioning and motion for each exercise. Improper form can lead to serious injury.

Biceps Curl

Targeted muscles: biceps

Equipment needed: dumbbells or resistance band

Procedure: Stand comfortably with your legs shoulder-width apart. Grasp a dumbbell in each hand, palms facing forward. Bend your arms at the elbow, curling your arms up until the dumbbells reach shoulder height. Slowly lower to the starting position.

Tips: Make sure you are lifting the appropriate amount of weight. This motion should use only the biceps muscle. Do not swing your upper body or use your shoulders and back to lift the weight. Proper form is essential. Using improper form, too much weight, or both will cause injuries.

Triceps Kickback

Targeted muscles: triceps

Equipment needed: dumbbells or resistance band

Procedure: Stand in a slight lunge with a dumbbell in your working hand. Bend your working arm at the elbow to a 90-degree angle. Slowly press your lower arm back until your arm is almost straight. Do not swing your arm. Keep your upper arm stable against your body. Slowly return to the starting position. Perform the correct number for a set on one side and then change sides.

Military Press

Targeted muscles: anterior, medial, and posterior deltoids; trapezius; triceps

Equipment needed: dumbbells or resistance band

Procedure: Stand with your legs hip-width apart, your abdominal muscles contracted, and a dumbbell in each hand. Lift weights to shoulder height with the palms facing forward. Slowly press the dumbbells to arm's length above your head, pause, then slowly lower to shoulder height to complete one repetition. (Warning: Do not perform this exercise if you have high blood pressure or a lower back problem.)

Single-Arm Row

Targeted muscles: latissimus dorsi, biceps

Equipment needed: dumbbells or resistance band

Procedure: Stand with your left knee and hand on your exercise bench, your right arm extended toward the floor, and a dumbbell in your right hand. Slowly pull the dumbbell toward your chest, leading with your elbow and keeping your arm close to your body. Pause; then lower the dumbbell back toward the ground to arm's length. This is one repetition on the right side. Complete a set on the right side and then switch to the left side (right knee and hand on the bench, left arm extended with a dumbbell). Alternate sets on each side.

Pectoral Fly

Targeted muscles: chest muscles (pectorals)

Equipment needed: dumbbells or resistance band and a bench or aerobic step

Procedure: Lie on your back with your knees bent, feet flat on the bench or floor, a dumbbell in each hand, and elbows bent. Keep your back flat on the bench or step throughout the exercise. Press the dumbbells toward the ceiling, hold for a count of 1, and return to the starting position for one repetition. Complete 8 to 12 repetitions for one set. Rest between sets. Complete two to three sets total. For a variation, from a standing position, use the same motion with the resistance band behind your back. Ends in your hands, press arms forward.

Crunch

Targeted muscles: abdominal muscles

Equipment needed: exercise mat, towel

Procedure: Lie on your back, knees bent, feet flat on the floor. Place the folded towel under the back of your head and grasp the ends with both hands. The towel will provide support for your head and neck during the crunch. To perform a proper crunch, contract your abdominal muscles while simultaneously raising your shoulders and upper body off the floor approximately six to eight inches. Do not curl your head or neck. Hold for a count of 2 and release. Repeat 10 times for one set. Perform a total of two to three sets, resting for at least two minutes between sets.

Tip: Concentrate on raising your body using only your abdominal muscles; do not use your back or shoulders or momentum to raise your upper body. Perform the crunches slowly and at a steady pace. You may not be able to raise your upper body six to eight inches off the floor at first. Move as far as you can until you strengthen your abdominal muscles to perform a regular crunch.

Bow

Targeted muscles: lower back muscles

Equipment needed: exercise mat

Procedure: Lie on your belly, hands stretched above your head. Slowly lift your head and feet off the ground forming a bow with your body. Hold for a count of 3 to 5 and lower. Repeat five times for a set. Complete two sets with a two-minute rest between sets.

Squat

Targeted muscles: gluteus, quadriceps, hamstrings, calf muscles

Equipment needed: dumbbells or resistance band

Procedure: Stand with soft knees, legs hip-width apart. Grasp a dumbbell in each hand. Slowly bend your knees and lower your body. Push your hips back and never allow your knees to move forward over your toes. Lower as far down as you can go. Aim for a 90-degree bend in your knees. Your chest remains forward and your rear end and hips are pushed back. Hold for a count of 3 and slowly rise back up to the standing position.

Lunge

Targeted muscles: gluteus, quadriceps, hamstrings, calf

Equipment needed: dumbbells or resistance band

Procedure: Stand with one foot in front of the other. Grasp a dumbbell in each hand. Slowly bend both of your knees until your front leg forms a 90-degree angle at the knee. The back foot should rise up so you are balancing on your toe. Hold for a count of 3 and slowly stand back up. Perform a complete set with one foot forward and then repeat with the other foot forward.

Anatomy of the Shoulder

The shoulder is the most mobile joint in the entire body. The shoulder joint is a ball and socket joint that allows movement in all three planes of motion. The major bone structure of the shoulder consists of the clavicle (collarbone), the scapula, the humerus (the top bone of the arm), the vertebrae of the spine, and the rib cage. Many muscles act on the shoulder joint. The muscles can be divided into two categories: the major muscles and the rotator cuff muscles.

Five major superficial (close to the surface) muscles act on the shoulder joint resulting in arm and upper back movement (see figure 5.2). The largest of the

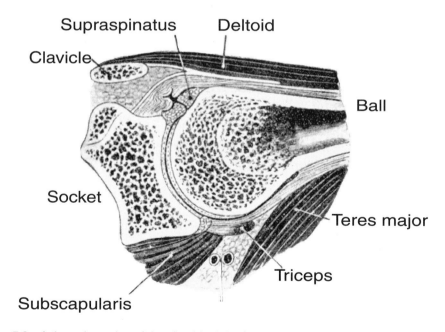

Figure 5.2 A through section of the shoulder joint (arm extended) showing all of the key bones and muscles of this ball and socket joint.

muscles are the muscles of the chest and the large muscles of the back. The muscles of the chest and back are antagonist muscles; they balance each other during the archery draw. You need to balance the development of antagonist muscles. An imbalance in strength between antagonist muscles can cause injury. The three remaining major muscles of the shoulder are the front, the side, and the back deltoids. These muscles must be developed equally to protect the shoulder joint during the repetition of the archery draw.

The rotator cuff muscles are a group of four small muscles deep in the shoulder joint. Even though these muscles are small, they hold and stabilize the arm when it is extended (e.g., during the movement of the archery draw). These muscles run between the upper arm and the back. The muscles are small and easily injured through overuse secondary to improper development and errors in training.

Rotator Cuff Injuries

The most common injury to the shoulder joint is *shoulder impingement syndrome*. Impingement syndrome is a very painful condition caused by the inflammation of the rotator cuff muscles. The rotator cuff muscles can swell and tear from overuse, lack of development, and improper form and training. As the syndrome progresses, the weakened and damaged muscles can cause inflammation of the bursa. The bursa are sacs in the joints containing fluid. During impingement syndrome, the bursa and inflamed muscles are pinched by the scapula when the arm or shoulder is moved. If left untreated, chronic bursitis and impingement syndrome can cause debilitating pain. If the archer "works through" the pain, permanent injury can result when the tendons are torn from their bony attachments. Surgery and extensive rehabilitation are required to repair the damage.

The initial symptom of impingement syndrome is pain when the arm is held over the head. Untreated impingement syndrome leads to pain when extending the arm forward (e.g., to shake hands). Pushing motions will also cause pain.

Treatment for impingement syndrome starts with rest. A physician should be consulted if the pain persists after an extended (two weeks) period of rest, if the pain has increased, or if the archer has had the pain for more than a month. Pushing movements must be avoided during the healing period.

If the damage to the rotator cuff is minor, the physician will prescribe a strength program for the entire shoulder, back, and chest. In addition, exercises specific to rotator cuff development will be added when the muscles have healed. If the damage is severe and involves tearing of the tendons, the only recourse may be surgery. Rotator cuff injury can be prevented by strengthening the rotator cuff muscles, the shoulder, and the chest and back muscles and by following a complete flexibility program.

Rotator Cuff Exercises

Perform the following exercises using light weights (one to three pounds) or a light resistance band. The rotator cuff muscles are small and relatively under-developed. Too much weight or incorrect form will lead to injury. Rotator cuff exercises should be done three times a week during the gain cycle, four times a week during the endurance cycle, and once a week during the maintenance cycle.

External Rotation

Targeted muscles: infraspinatus and the teres minor

Procedure: Lie on your side with your elbow close to your ribs. Grasp the dumbbell in your hand. Slowly raise the dumbbell until it is pointed to the ceiling. Do not move your elbow away from your body. Pause before slowly lowering the dumbbell back to the starting position.

Internal Rotation

Targeted muscles: subscapularis

Procedure: Lie on your back. Grasp a weight with your arm bent at the elbow. Your elbow should remain close to the side of your body. Slowly rotate your arm, raising the dumbbell toward the ceiling. Pause before slowly lowering the dumbbell back to the starting position.

Inverted Arm Raise

Targeted muscles: supraspinatus

Procedure: Stand comfortably grasping a dumbbell in each hand. This exercise is done with a straight elbow and with the thumb pointing *down*. Instead of lifting your arms straight out to the sides, hold your arms approximately 30 degrees forward of a straight side lift. Lift your arms about two-thirds of the distance to shoulder level. Do not lift your arms up to shoulder height. Slowly lower to the starting position.

Tip: This exercise must be performed properly to work the supraspinatus. The positioning of the arms, the thumb, and the lift are important. Work on perfect form while doing this exercise.

Flexibility Training

The final element of a well-balanced fitness program is flexibility. Flexibility exercises increase the range of motion of the joints, elongate the muscles, provide a warm-up and cool-down of the body, and decrease the risk of injury. A stretching program should include a series of slow stretches of each body part. Flexibility is especially important for archers. Archery practice usually involves shooting hundreds of arrows over extended periods. Archers spend most of their training and competition day on their feet, frozen in their archery stance, which causes the muscles to cool down and shorten. To maintain optimum muscle performance, archers should stretch at least once an hour during competitions and training. A comprehensive postworkout stretching program increases the range of motion of the joints and is the perfect way to relax the body and mind after a long day of training.

A flexible joint has a complete range of motion (ROM). ROM is defined as the ability of a joint to move freely in every direction. Joint mobility is limited by the joint structure, the elasticity and strength of the surrounding muscles, and the connective tissue of the joint. Flexibility training minimizes these factors. Like other aspects of physical conditioning, ROM can be improved with a complete flexibility training program.

Warming Up

Before performing any stretching activity, warm up the muscles. Your warm-up should consist of any slow, rhythmic exercise employing the major muscle groups. Marching in place while pumping the arms, fast walking, light jogging, and rhythmic dancing are all examples of warm-up movement. A minimum of 10 minutes of warm-up exercises must be performed before starting the full body stretching program described here. Warming up increases the blood flow to the muscles, making them pliable and more receptive to stretching. An inadequate warm-up increases the risk of injury and painful muscles.

Each of these stretches can be performed after a proper warm-up. All movement should be slow and controlled. Exhale as you perform the stretch and hold each stretch for 15 to 20 seconds. Only stretch as far as you can comfortably. Never force a stretch. Do not bounce. A properly performed stretch should not cause pain. If you feel pain, stop immediately. Warm joints and muscles will stretch more readily.

Stretching Technique

Whole body stretching should be performed daily. Always stretch each body part you have used during an exercise session. Use the rest time between weightlifting sets to stretch the body part used. Remember to stretch between ends when shooting. Studies have shown that stretching in conjunction with muscle toning exercise will increase the benefits of the exercise. In other words, if you stretch while you lift weights, you will achieve better results.

Hip Flexor Stretch

Targeted muscles: muscles of the hip, upper leg, and lower back

Procedure: Start this stretch by kneeling on one knee with the other knee bent and the foot flat out in front. Gently lean forward into the extended knee, stretching the hip flexors. Hold the stretch before changing sides. You should feel this stretch in your hip muscles and lower back.

Lying Hamstring Stretch

Targeted muscles: hamstring muscles of the leg and the lower back

Procedure: Lie on your back with your knees bent and your feet flat on the floor. Straighten your right leg and lift it perpendicular to your body. Grasp your right leg and pull it gently toward your body. Hold for a count of 10 and release. Switch sides. Perform three times per side.

Quadriceps Stretch

Targeted muscles: quadriceps muscles

Procedure: Stand on your left leg, bend your right leg behind you at the knee, and grasp your foot with your right hand (hold onto a chair for stabilization). Hold this position for a count of 10. You should feel the stretch in the front of your bent leg. Repeat on the left side.

Calf Stretch

Targeted muscles: calf muscles

Procedure: Stand with your feet together. Step your right foot out in front of you, bend your knee slightly, and push the heel of your back foot into the ground. Feel the stretch in the calf muscles of your back leg. Hold for a count of 10. Repeat on the other side.

Back Stretch

Targeted muscles: shoulder muscles, muscles on the side of the abdomen, muscles of the back and chest

Procedure: Stand with your feet hip-width apart. Reach your right arm over your head. Gently bend to the left side, holding the stretch for a count of 10. Change the stretch by reaching to the side and forward (approximately to an 11 o'clock position) and hold. Repeat on the right side, reaching with your left arm for the side stretch. Reach toward the 1 o'clock position for the forward stretch. You should feel this stretch in your lower back.

Shoulder Stretch

Targeted muscles: shoulder muscles, muscles of the upper back and chest

Procedure: Cross your right arm over the front of your body and grasp your right arm with your left hand at the elbow. Gently push your right arm toward your body, stretching the shoulder muscles of your right arm. Hold for a count of 10 and repeat on the left side. Perform this stretch at least twice on each side.

Upper Back Stretch

Targeted muscles: upper back and chest muscles

Procedure: Clasp your hands in front of your body, palms facing away from you. Push your hands forward, feeling the stretch in your upper back and shoulders. Hold for a count of 10. Clasp your hands behind your back, palms facing toward you. Push your hands away from you and gently stretch your upper back. Hold for a count of 10. Perform both stretches three times.

Inverted V Stretch

Targeted muscles: This stretch benefits the entire body starting with the upper and lower back, the shoulders, the hips, the hamstrings, the calves, and the heel and foot.

Procedure: Lie on your belly on an exercise mat with your hands stretched out in front of you. Push yourself up into an inverted V. (You can also enter this position by bending forward from a standing position to form an inverted V.) Hold this position for a full minute, stretching your back and legs. Relax into the stretch and concentrate on your breathing. Release and repeat.

Getting the Edge on the Competition

A complete training program is an integral part of an archer's training. Improvements in strength, flexibility, and cardiovascular conditioning will allow you to train on the range for longer periods of time while reducing your risk of injury. A strong, flexible body will enable you to recover from injuries more quickly. A conditioning program is also a good way to clear your mind and concentrate on activities other than archery, the shot, the rankings, and the upcoming competition. You can improve your technique, your scores, and your health and life by making conditioning a daily part of your archery training.

Tuning the Mind

Lisa Franseen, PhD

The beauty and fun of archery is that it can be enjoyed on many levels, from spending a couple of days a year shooting with some buddies to devoting one's life to the sport. Americans learning the sport of archery usually begin with form and execution (thus, where *Precision Archery* begins). Many archers choose to stop there, whereas others have a curiosity and drive to explore other ways to enhance their skills. Whether it is through equipment and tuning, coaching, or physical conditioning and fitness, the learning process can be endless. More important, it is fun and inspiring!

Likewise, learning the role that the mind plays in the game of archery can be fascinating and has led many archers to excel. Accomplished archers will say that shooting is at least 70 percent mental (some even say it is 99 percent!). Although the actual percentage is up for debate, the mind clearly plays an important role. On its own, the mind is quite undisciplined. It thinks whatever it wants to all day long. The mind has the potential to lead even the most talented shooter to perform inconsistently, to lose focus, to choke under pressure, to freeze at full draw, to wallow in self-hatred for getting "only" second place, and worse, to quit the sport entirely. At its best, however, the mind can produce a transcendent performance.

Just as the body develops a habit of shooting in a particular way, the mind develops habits of thinking, attitude, perception and interpretation, and reaction during the shot. Our particular habits can indeed work against us and lead us to feel powerless, especially if we're not aware of them. After years of doing sport psychology with archers, beginners to elite, I have found that those archers who know the role their minds play are better able to use them to their own advantage. The key to that advantage is to develop a disciplined mind through awareness, mental skills training, and practice. In doing so, you can break your bad mental habits, develop habits that work for you rather than against you, and find more success.

A Word on the Unconscious

Several sources in sport psychology literature address the role of the unconscious in sport performance (Bassham 1995; Gallwey 1998; Honda and Newson 1972). The issue, and confusion around it, is often broached at my coaching certification workshops. Commonly asked questions include: Do we shoot with the unconscious? Are the unconscious and subconscious different? What is the role of the conscious? How do the two interact? Is conscious shooting always bad?

The confusion is semantic. The words *unconscious, subconscious,* and *conscious* are fraught with misunderstanding. For purposes of clarity, my own personal approach is to assume that the unconscious and subconscious are similar enough to avoid differentiation and to replace them with the term *physical/intuitive*. I then replace the word *conscious* with *mental awareness*. Let's begin by looking at the role of each during the execution of a strong shot.

Your physical body is trained to execute a shot in a particular way. Mental awareness is most required during the initial learning process. For example, at first we must remind ourselves constantly of what we're doing (Okay, I need to rotate my elbow out so I don't whack it when I release the string). Gradually, through practice and repetition, this physical response will occur automatically without mental awareness. Physical precision is also guided by our intuition. With each draw, a decision is made as to when to release the arrow. This decision comes in an instant, and we know it intuitively. That is, if we stop and think of the release (Now? Should I release now? . . . or now?), the intuitive moment is lost and the release is forced.

For experienced archers, the execution of a shot requires only an automatic physical response guided by intuition. Mental awareness is only needed for keeping track of the process (e.g., which bow to pick up at the start of a new end, which target to shoot at, how many arrows are left to shoot, and from which direction the wind is blowing), for making corrections (I need to change my sight), and for providing reminders of skills on which we're working (reinforcing key concepts such as back tension or relaxed bow hand).

When mental awareness gets in the way of our physical or intuitive process, it's time for mind tuning.

Identifying the Mind's Role

Psychological influences cause physiological changes, such as increased heart rate, muscle tension, sweaty palms, upset stomach, or shallow breathing, which cause changes in the execution of your shot. Changes in your shot commonly lead to mental reactions such as worry, dread, focusing on past mistakes or future negative possibilities, a loss of confidence, or increased frustration. Here are some questions that can help you identify these psychological influences:

- Is your performance in practice better than in competition?
- Do you get overly nervous for competition?
- Do you criticize yourself for making mistakes?
- Do things around you easily distract you?
- Do you ever dread competition and wish it could just be over and done with?
- Are you too relaxed and indifferent when you shoot?
- Do you get angry easily when shooting isn't going how you'd like?
- Do you get distracted at key points in competition?
- Is motivating for practice difficult?

Each of the preceding questions addresses issues related to your mind. If you answered yes to any of them, some thought, perception, belief system, or attitude is interfering with your body's ability to shoot the way it has been trained to shoot. Figure 6.1 illustrates the vicious cycle that can occur.

Day-to-day fluctuations in our performances are caused primarily by psychological factors; physical abilities are relatively stable (Weinberg and Gould 1995). Athletes who can focus on the task at hand and be consumed only by the present moment express true physical abilities. Mihalyi Csikszentmihalyi (1975) called this state "flow." Many others call it "the zone." The feeling is of effortless movement (like performing on autopilot), a merging of action and awareness, a loss of self-consciousness, and a sense of control (Weinberg and Gould 1995). "Flow" is a perfect example of the mind working for us, rather than getting in our way.

Getting out of your own way, as it may be called, then, means literally to learn and practice skills to prevent your mind from having a negative influence on your performance. Sport psychology has called these skills mental skills, and their

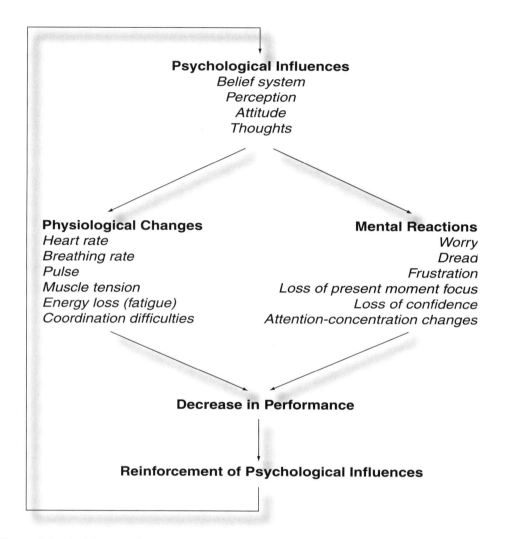

Figure 6.1 A vicious cycle can start with a thought or a deed (Oh no, I shot a 5!). What follows—a thought or attitude (I know I wasn't going to shoot a personal best today!) leads to physical and mental reactions (heart racing, frustration) which leads to lower performance leading to . . .

effectiveness is supported by a vast amount of research. Through mental skills, an archer can control nervousness levels, maintain focus, decrease distractibility, increase motivation, control emotions, stay positive, accelerate the learning process, and improve already learned skills.

Anyone who is interested can learn to discipline the mind and use it to advantage through mental skills training. Young children certainly have the ability to learn simple techniques. Mental skills for beginners, learned early in the process of shooting, can help prevent the development of bad mental habits. Coaches are also highly advised to teach their students mental skills or to employ an expert to do so.

Anxiety and Performance

An archer's level of arousal and anxiety is a variable in shooting performance. Arousal can vary on a continuum from deeply relaxed to panic. The higher your level of arousal, the faster your heart beats, the more tense your muscles, the more upset your stomach, and the more shallow your breathing.

Mental anxiety increases physiological anxiety. Situational stress is one contributor to mental anxiety. Two examples are the importance of the event and the degree of uncertainty about the outcome or others' feelings and evaluations (Martens 1987). Some people tend to perceive situations with more anxiety in general. Such people are more likely to perceive competition as threatening. Low self-esteem lends itself to low self-confidence. Going into a challenging situation, such as a tournament, with low self-confidence tends to increase a person's anxiety.

Each archer has an optimal level of physiological arousal that leads to his or her best performances. Figure 6.2 (Landers and Boutcher 1986) shows how very low and very high anxiety lead to poorer performances; an arousal level somewhere between low and high leads to peak performances. Everyone has an optimal level of anxiety. Some perform best when they are more relaxed; some perform best when they are more aroused; and a few perform best on either end of the continuum.

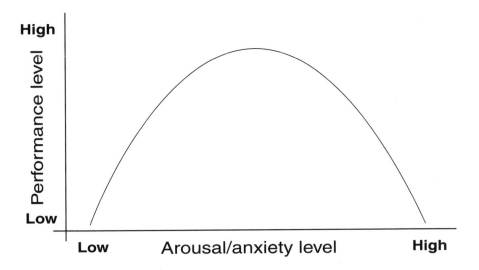

Figure 6.2 Both high arousal or anxiety levels (I have to win!!) and low arousal levels (Whatever.) lead to poor performances. Your personal optimal arousal/anxiety level must be determined.

Finding Your Optimal Level

What is your optimal arousal level? Think back on your best performance. Close your eyes and imagine yourself shooting, how it felt, and then rate on a scale of 1 to 10 how relaxed or anxious you were (1 = extremely relaxed or flat; 10 = extremely anxious or panicked). Now rate how relaxed or anxious you were as you think back on your worst performance. Monitor yourself over a couple of weeks by rating your anxiety level after each practice and each competition and comparing it to your performance level. See if you can identify the level of arousal at which you perform best. Keeping a logbook may help (see figure 6.3).

You can learn skills to help control your level of physiological arousal, including deep breathing, relaxation, psyching-up methods, imagery, self-talk, and effective goal setting. Many sport psychology books available today make reference to these mental skills with helpful, detailed information and illustrations. My sport psychology articles in *Archery Focus* magazine also address these skills in much more depth (see For More Information on page 183).

Deep Breathing

Deep breathing is one of the most effective ways to control anxiety and muscle tension. As pressure and stress increase, as in tournament situations, many competitors either hold their breath or take short, shallow breaths. Both of these reactions are associated with increased muscle tension. Deep breathing can lead to a greater sense of stability and centeredness (Nideffer 1985). Because you can think about only one thing at a time, focusing on your breathing takes your mind off potentially interfering distractions, such as your opponent, your score, or your place in the competition.

To practice deep breathing, the in-breath should occur through the nose and last about three to five seconds; the out-breath should occur through the mouth and last about five to seven seconds. When inhaling, breathe from the diaphragm. Exhale slowly and steadily. Toward the end of the exhalation, employ a slight "squeezing" of the diaphragm. Many good sources, especially yoga and meditation literature, can give you more detailed instruction on breathing techniques.

Relaxation Training

The goal of daily or weekly training in relaxation is to learn to relax your body and mind completely in a very short time. What at first takes 20 or 30 minutes to accomplish can soon take only a minute or two. This way, relaxation can be used on the spot during tournaments when you need to decrease your level of physiological arousal. Relaxation has other benefits in addition to decreasing overall arousal levels. It enhances your awareness of even slight changes in muscle tension. This body awareness can be helpful during competition. As with deep breathing, relaxation also quiets the mind. The concentration required makes

ANXIETY LEVEL LOGBOOK

Date: _____

Practice or competition (circle one)

Comments

I felt: (circle one)

    Extremely relaxed, flat   1   2   3   4   5   6   7   8   9   10   Extremely anxious, panicked

Comments

Performance level: (circle one)

               Poor   1   2   3   4   5   6   7   8   9   10   Excellent

Comments

Figure 6.3 A sample page from a logbook useful in monitoring your arousal/anxiety level.

this exercise very helpful in stopping ineffective thinking patterns and bringing you back to the present moment. Take a look at the following general guidelines for relaxation training.

1. Find a quiet place free from distractions (such as the phone, television, and other people).
2. Get into a comfortable sitting position; feel free to move about as you relax to get more comfortable. Lying down may be too relaxing and lead to sleep.
3. Begin with breathing and proceed only once your breathing is relaxed, deep, and even.
4. Use focusing devices such as a relaxation tape or a coach to lead you through the process.
5. Allow any random thoughts or images to enter your mind and to pass through without attending to them.

There are two forms of relaxation training techniques. In *active relaxation* you focus on all of the major areas and muscles groups throughout your body one by one (toes, feet, arches, ankles, shins, calves, thighs, hamstrings, buttocks, abdomen), actively tensing each area while focusing on the sensation of tension, and then actively releasing the tension to allow the area to "let go" and feel more relaxed. *Passive relaxation* is similar; however, you just focus on "allowing" (i.e., not forcing) the muscle groups to release themselves. Focus on the sensation you are trying to create and add relaxing self-talk, repeated slowly and methodically, such as, *My legs are feeling heavier and heavier, warmer and warmer . . .*

Imagery

Imagery, or visualization, is a powerful mental tool with a number of benefits. A vast amount of scientific research shows that imagery helps to improve performance; it can strengthen already learned skills, maintain skills during injury, and enhance the learning of new skills. Imagery can help you prepare psychologically for competition, relax, or "psych up." Focusing on what you want, whether it is more motivation, self-confidence, or positive emotion, will help you to achieve it. The reason is that imagery pulls your thoughts away from negativity and other damaging images. A by-product of imagery is that it enhances focusing abilities because it requires a concentrated effort.

Imagery can be compared to a dress rehearsal. Going through a performance or some skill in your mind serves as a rehearsal, or practice, for the real thing. The more you rehearse, the better your actual performance will be. Research has shown that visualizing an activity in your mind can induce the same physiological response as actually performing that activity, although to a lesser degree. Theoretically, then, for archery, imagining yourself pulling back the arrow should cause slight neuromuscular impulses in your back muscles. It is a way of programming your muscles to perform more automatically.

As with any other skill, effective imagery takes time. With practice you will find it easier to control what you're imagining, and the image will be more life-like. Use all of your senses—color, direct light and shadow, odors such as grass on the shooting field, sensations such as the sun on your back, and sounds such as arrows being released and hitting targets. Include both physical and emotional feelings (your arm guard on your forearm, the weight of your bow) as well as your overall mood and perhaps a bit of nervousness. The more detailed the imagery, the better.

Self-Talk Techniques

The only thing that is happening is right now—at this very moment in time. The moment is gone in an instant, and then we have the next moment. Best performances come when we are absorbed in the present moment. Much of what we talk to ourselves about, however, is in the past, in the form of self-criticism and regret, or in the future, in the form of anticipation and worry. Likewise, thinking about our score, other shooters, our place, our growling stomach, or some rude comment someone just made all serve to pull our focus away from the moment. Learning to control self-talk is one of the most powerful ways of tuning the mind and making it work for us rather than against us.

The list of not-in-the-moment thoughts is endless! Thankfully, effective ways to return to the present are available. I've already discussed the power of deep breathing, relaxation, and imagery for such purposes. Here are some additional techniques:

- *Thought stopping.* Thought stopping requires awareness that you are thinking something unproductive to the task at hand. Once you catch yourself saying it, firmly say "Stop!" and have an already planned thought to take its place (see the next two techniques).

- *Positive self-statements and cue words.* Positive self-statements are created to train the mind to be positive and to make reality out of dreams. They are said repeatedly throughout the day. McKinney gives a great review with examples in *The Simple Art of Winning* (Leo Planning Inc., 1996). Cue words are one-word self-statements that have the intent of triggering an action or feeling. *Smooth, calm, now,* and *patience* are examples. Say both self-statements and cue words with vigor, as though you really mean it; this changes the physiology that accompanies the thought. If you find, after using a statement over time, that you are having difficulty saying it with vigor, then it may have lost its power and it is time to create a new one.

- *Detachment.* Remember that you are not your thoughts. For many reasons that I won't discuss here, your mind is creating nonsense. Don't buy into it!

Detachment involves taking a step back from the interfering thought, seeing it for what it is, and letting it go.

Goal Setting

Effective goal setting increases focus, motivation, direction, feelings of success, and self-confidence. All of that equals more fun! Helpful goals also have certain characteristics that Gould (1993) discusses in detail. They are as follow:

- Realistic yet challenging
- Specific
- Stated in the positive
- Stated actively, not passively
- Written down
- Evaluated periodically
- Individual commitment to reach goal
- Supported by significant others

Goals should be set for each season (both indoor and outdoor), reviewed each month, and changed to be more realistic or challenging when necessary. Goals should also be set for each day in practice, as well as each tournament. Daily goals depend on what you need to do at that time to reach your season goals. Using a daily training log, organized in a notebook with an attached pen, helps assure that you will develop this productive habit (see figure 6.4).

A very common mistake is to set only *outcome goals* and to forget about *process goals*. Outcome goals tend to focus on your place or score in a competition. Process goals focus more on immediate, here-and-now behaviors performed with each shot, or even between shots. They also include mental goals such as, *I will take a deep breath before every shot in the elimination rounds.* Process goals give you specific here-and-now things to focus on, whereas outcome goals are just things we hope to accomplish.

To be sure you are setting process goals, ask yourself, *How will I accomplish that?* For example, let's say that one of your goals is to win your state championship. How will you accomplish that? Add another goal to answer this, such as, *Place in the top three in all tournaments leading up to the state championship.* How will you accomplish that? Goal: *Increase my focus by 30 percent.* How will you accomplish that? Goal: *Focus on back tension and a relaxed bow hand.* Take a deep breath before every shot. And so forth. Another common mistake is to neglect evaluating your progress toward your goals. Figure 6.5 is an example of a postcompetition evaluation. Evaluate your performance, physically and psychologically, after every tournament.

Part of goal setting is developing a mental program or a planned and specific way of incorporating mental skills training into practice and competition. If you forget this step, it is easy to forget about mind tuning altogether! Devote days

DAILY TRAINING LOG

Date _____

Before-Practice Plan

Today in practice, I want to work on the following things:

Task goal 1: _____

Task goal 2: _____

Mental goal: _____

Before-Practice Plan

1	2	3	4	5
Don't want to practice		Average motivation		Can't wait to start

Comments: _____

After-Practice Comments

Did you meet your goals for today? Check the one that closest matches how you did:

Goal 1:	1	2	3	4	5
	Met 0% goal		Met 50% goal		Met 100% goal

Goal 2:	1	2	3	4	5
	Met 0% goal		Met 50% goal		Met 100% goal

Mental Goal:	1	2	3	4	5
	Met 0% goal		Met 50% goal		Met 100% goal

Self-Talk

What were you saying to yourself during training?

_____

Energy Level

How much energy did you have today?

1	2	3	4	5
No energy				Very high energy

Name at least one positive thing you did today in practice:

_____

Name at least one thing you really want to keep working on:

_____

Figure 6.4 A sample training log page structured for goal assessment. A logbook can greatly help you in creating productive habits.

POSTCOMPETITION EVALUATION

At my last competition, I think I did:

      1   2   3   4   5

Horribly   Incredibly well

No matter how I did overall, I did these three things well:

1.

2.

3.

I learned these three things:

1.

2.

3.

I need to work on these three things:

1.

2.

3.

Figure 6.5 A sample page from a post-competition evaluation logbook. If you don't evaluate yourself, who will?

PRECOMPETITION MENTAL PLAN

When preparing for competition, decide what thoughts, feelings, images, and physical movements help you best when getting ready to perform. Draw on what has worked well for you in the past and what seems to be associated with your best performances. Some examples are mental imagery, cue words, positive self-statements and affirmations, competition goals, desired mood, psyching-up strategy or relaxation strategy, and key things to focus on.

The night before:

The morning of the competition:

General warm-up (physical and mental):

Official practice:

Prestart, immediate preparation (include adjustments in optimal energy level):

During morning competition:

Figure 6.6 What you learn from past performances becomes the focus for the mental plans for your next competition.

of practice specifically to mind tuning. Make a refocusing plan to use at times in competition when you have lost your focus or when things are not going the way you had hoped. Write the plan down on index cards. Have it in your bow case or in your quiver for quick reference. Visualize yourself effectively using your plan. The refocus plan can be part of a precompetition mental plan that many archers have used to assure that they are physically and psychologically ready for a tournament (see figure 6.6).

Creating an Environment for Success

In addition to developing the mental skills just discussed, your practice environment is key in creating mind-tuning opportunities. Always practicing in "perfect" conditions is not adequate preparation for the pressures and distractions of competition. You should be shooting in the rain; in intense heat and freezing cold; in swirling, gusty winds blowing from the left, the right, behind, and head on. Shoot elimination rounds with lights, timers, and whistles. Be creative with other shooters and create pressures similar to competition, such as shooting for score with exaggerated distractions.

What about those days when you really, really don't want to practice or it feels as though you've completely forgotten how to shoot? These are the best mental training days you'll ever find. Stay positive, regardless of the scores. Don't whine or blame. Shoot with enthusiasm and "fake it" if you must. Pretend to be confident. Attempt to be amused and entertained. Accept that some days are not how we'd like them to be. Practicing having this positive frame of mind will make it easier in challenging competitions.

One area to assess is your relationships (Coppel 1995; Hellstedt 1995). Are your parents or spouse putting too much pressure on you to win? Is your spouse upset at how much time you are spending away? Is your coach giving all of his attention to another student? Are the other kids in the JOAD program unjustly picking on, or ignoring, you? Another area to assess is the demands from other parts of your life, such as work deadlines, final exams, child-rearing responsibilities, potential divorce or the recent death of a loved one, medical complications, financial strain, the effects of drug abuse, depression, and other stressors.

If something in the environment is interfering, then it's time to give it attention. It is also helpful to remember that you cannot control what occurs externally; you can only control your reaction to it. Not giving it your direct attention too often leads to reactions (e.g., frustration, anger, fatigue, burnout, loss of focus) that exacerbate the problem. Rather than be reactive, you can be proactive. You can take responsibility for what is yours to change and work to let go of what you cannot change.

Even though a problem lies outside of you, you must look at what you can do to address it. Blaming something or someone else does nothing to change it and only serves to make you see yourself as a victim. If you cannot change the situation, you can ask for help in coping with it, adopt a new perspective to change your reaction to it and thus your behavior, set more realistic goals that take into account the whole picture, or take time off.

Heightening Your Mental Toughness

Beyond practicing basic mental skills you may be interested in advanced mind tuning. This is suitable if you are competing at a high level, in a slump or experiencing a psychological condition such as target panic, experiencing a plateau but want to continue to improve, bored with just shooting arrows and feel no direction, or just interested or more psychologically minded by nature.

Great archers are extremely consistent in performance regardless of external circumstances. Whether shooting alone in their backyards or in front of thousands at the Olympics, they remain focused and repeatedly shoot the same shot over and over, one at a time. To do this requires precision of mental control practiced diligently over the years and a deep commitment to *use* all of the challenges that arise as opportunities to retrain the mind. Without some type of mind tuning, good archers cannot become great.

Just as awareness builds on what a good shot feels like and how to change a bad shot back to a good shot, a mentally tough archer builds awareness of a positive frame of mind and how to change a negative frame back to a positive one. For example, a good shooter knows almost immediately when something has changed in the execution of a shot: *I dropped my bow hand, My string hand is tense, My back tension wasn't right,* and so on. Likewise, a mentally tough archer recognizes distraction and knows when to take a deep, slow breath, let go of frustration, and refocus on the cue word.

The following are what I call "perspectives of excellence" and are sure to help you pave your way to reaching your potential. Each addresses one critical aspect of the mental landscape of competition.

1. **Redefine Winning and Embrace True Success**

   In a sport-crazed and competitive society such as the United States, it is difficult to get away from attitudes shown in expressions such as, First place is the only place, or, Second place is the first place loser. When you hear, How did you do? you assume the person is asking if you won, what place you got, or what your score was. This obsession with outcome is exactly what keeps many athletes from reaching their potential.

   What does it really mean to win? A new definition is in order. Winning is personal. It happens when you overcome an obstacle within yourself. It is beating the very obstacles you often put in front of yourself. It is focusing on the process when all else says to focus on the outcome. It is persevering beyond where most are willing. It is continuing to love yourself despite being in "last place."

In line with winning, society too often labels the winners as successful and the "losers" as, well, losers—unsuccessful failures who are looked down on as "not having what it takes." We recognize *true* success, however, not by looking at how an archer shoots when the going is easy, but when it is challenging. Success is the ability to have fun no matter how seriously the sport is being taken. Success is learning from failure and adversity rather than allowing it to make you feel inferior or making excuses for it.

2. **Change Your Perspective**

   Human beings like to be right, and that includes being right about their perspectives or their interpretations of why things are the way they are. Perspectives can keep us from moving forward, however, and are often worth changing. Seeing something in a new way has the power to change or shift what seemed impossible.

   To take an example, if you have hit a performance plateau, are currently in a slump, or are experiencing target panic, then you are most likely frustrated, feeling a little helpless to change it, and wondering why in the world this is happening to you. What purpose does it have? Consider another perspective. Without eventually incorporating mental awareness into your game, you are not likely to reach your true potential. And, like most human beings, you aren't going to do something until you have to. Thus, your plateau or slump or target panic is the very thing that can finally motivate you to explore the role of the mind. Perhaps your current frustration is less a frustration and more a gift. With this new perspective, your "problem" will probably still be frustrating, but there is purpose in it and you are no longer a victim of it. That perspective alone can make a huge difference and move you out of your problem more quickly.

3. **Go With and Not Against Adversity**

   As aikido and many other martial arts teach us, we are much more likely to reach the results we want when we go *with* difficult situations and not *against* them. This attitude encompasses a gentle, forgiving approach to learning and making mistakes, rather than an aggressive, critical one. It emphasizes not taking anything personally, not anyone, any situation, or even ourselves. It underscores the importance of detaching ourselves from our emotions, good or bad, so we can remain objective, clear, and precise. Going with adversity means accepting ourselves for where we are (in this case, how we're performing) while continuing to strive for excellence.

Good luck with your mental tuning. As Rick McKinney said in chapter 1, "competition . . . involves taking chances and learning, learning about your sport, but more important, *learning about yourself.*" If you take to heart some of the ideas in this chapter and incorporate them into your training, you may reach the next level!

7

Tuning Recurve Bows and Arrows

Don Rabska

There is no doubt that the recurve bow you choose is an important consideration in how well you can shoot, but even more important than the bow are the arrows you choose. Remember, it is not the bow scoring the points in the target; it is your arrows. Successful bow tuning and accurate shooting can only be achieved by using arrow shafts that are properly spined to your bow and ones that are consistent in their spine, weight, and straightness. Just about every top archer in the world uses Easton® arrows, but that final shaft selection is up to you. The true verification that you have selected the correct spine will be determined during the tuning process. Problems caused by improperly spined arrow shafts will become evident during tuning. Before tuning, be sure that all of your arrows are straight and properly fletched and have perfectly aligned nocks.

Your shooting technique has a large influence over the dynamic spine of your arrow—that is, how it behaves in flight. Two archers shooting the same bow, draw weight, and arrow length may not necessarily shoot the same arrow size. Usually, the archer who has better "line" (see chapter 3 for details on body alignment) will shoot a lighter (weaker) spined arrow than an archer who has poor skeletal alignment. This is because the archer with good alignment creates less side movement of the string on release, resulting in less flexing of the arrow shaft.

Before starting the bow tuning process, install every piece of equipment on your bow that you intend to use during shooting. This includes the correct bowstring and all attachments to the bowstring, bow sight, stabilizers, arrow rest, cushion plunger, counter weights, and so on. Use all personal items as well, such as your tab, chest protector, and anything else you use when shooting. Any adjustments made to the bow or changes in bow components can, and usually will, affect the tune.

Once your equipment is fully assembled, the next phase in the process of achieving well-tuned equipment is good preliminary setup. If the initial setup is done properly, the tuning process can be accomplished with little effort.

Adjustments made to the bow, changes in bow components, or alterations in shooting form can affect the tune or your equipment. Any change to either will produce varying results. During the tuning process, it is vitally important that you change only one variable at a time. Otherwise, you will have a very difficult time determining which adjustment caused any grouping changes. If, after trying all of the tuning adjustments outlined in this chapter, your arrows still do not fly true, you may need to change your arrow size to a stiffer or weaker shaft and retune.

Preliminary Setup of the Bow

Before you can begin tuning your recurve bow, you must put the bow into a reasonable starting point. Here are the steps.

Installing the Nocking Point

Install a moveable nocking point on the bowstring. As an example of the critical nature of bowstring mass (the physical weight of the bowstring), a simple metal nocking point that weighs between three and five grains will have a similar effect on the dynamic spine of the arrow as if you had changed your bow weight by one to two pounds! Therefore, use the same type of nocking point you intend to shoot normally. Initially, position the nocking point on the bowstring about 1/2 inch (1.3 centimeters) above square (see figure 7.1). During the tuning process, the nocking point will most likely be moved lower, but this is a good starting point.

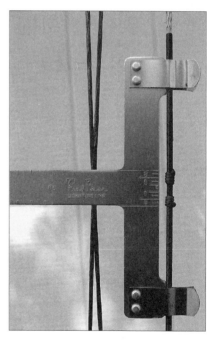

Figure 7.1 A starting point for the position of your nocking point indicator is about one half inch above square (square being the bottom edge of the bow square which is sitting on the bow's arrow rest).

Finding the Limb Centers

Finding and marking the exact centers of the limbs of your recurve bow will give you reference points from which to adjust your arrow's left-right position on the bow. To find the limb centers on a recurve bow, place a piece of masking tape across the inside of each limb about 6 inches (15 centimeters) above the base of the riser (or use Beiter blocks, which are available from most good archery shops). Using the tape method, measure the width of each limb and make a small vertical mark on the tape in the exact center of each limb. Be very accurate when doing this, and measure several times to know you have located the exact center of each limb. This mark will be used for arrow centering (see figure 7.2).

Centering the Arrow

Centering the arrow means adjusting the arrow's left-right position. The objective of arrow centering is to have the arrow leave the

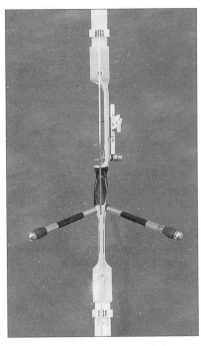

Figure 7.2 Beiter blocks can be clipped to the limbs a short distance above and below the riser to help you find your bow's limb centers. Alternatively, pieces of tape with marks in the center of each limb can be used.

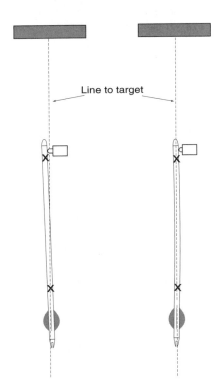

Line to target

bow through the "theoretical" or "balanced" limb center of the bow. To accomplish this, adjust the horizontal (in/out) position of the cushion plunger or arrow rest assembly so that the tip (center) of the arrow *point* is correctly aligned.

In reality, the two "nodes" of the arrow shaft should be in alignment to the target during the arrow's time in the air (see figure 7.3). Releasing the string with your fingers creates a horizontal bending motion within the arrow.

Figure 7.3 Because the finger release of a recurve bow imparts some sideways movement to the arrow, the arrow at rest generally protrudes out from the bow so that you can see the arrow point from behind the string *(a)*. If you line the arrow's nodes up directly with the target, you will impact to the right because the back node moves out from the bow upon the loose of the arrow *(b)*.

As the arrow oscillates during its flight path, the goal is to have the nodes remain in direct alignment to the target. Figure 7.3 clearly illustrates the front and rear node positions of the arrow. The front node is usually closer to the front end of the arrow than the rear node is to the nock end. This is due to the mass (weight) of the point.

Effects of the Finger Release

The finger release causes the bowstring to move toward the archer's bow shoulder on release. This creates horizontal bending or "column loading" of the shaft. It is also commonly referred to as "the archer's paradox." To compensate for this lateral movement of the string and arrow, the static position of the arrow should be set very slightly outside the vertical center of the bow. Align the "tip" of the arrow point about 1/16 inch (1.6 millimeters) or less outside the bowstring when viewed from behind the arrow with the bowstring properly centered. The arrow tip (the very tip of the arrow point) is placed slightly outside the string to provide compensation for the amount the cushion plunger or side-loading device compresses into the bow when the arrow is released (see figure 7.4). The horizontal force created by the finger release forces the arrow to first bend in toward the bow. Then, at the very moment

Figure 7.4 The white button behind the arrow is attached to a spring in the cushion plunger. It absorbs some of the sideways motion imparted by the finger release and hence can be used to tune arrow flight to some degree.

it completes this initial bend and starts the recovery bend, the cushion plunger depresses, and in the next moment the arrow shaft leaves the arrow rest. All of this action occurs in a fraction of a second in the first several inches of forward travel of the arrow.

In the next horizontal bending sequence, as the arrow leaves the cushion plunger and arrow rest, the arrow is in a nearly free mode; it is being held only by the bowstring during this second half cycle. At the end of this complete cycle (bending in toward, then bending away from, the bow), the arrow nock disengages from the bowstring, sending the arrow on its way to the target. The arrow is then on its way, freely oscillating all the way to the target. The amount of oscillation decreases as the arrow travels farther from the bow.

Aligning the Bow-Sight Pin

Initially, set the sight pin on your bow sight over the centerline of the arrow shaft. This is simply a good starting point; it is not likely to stay in this position. Some archers believe that the sight should end up over the center of the arrow for a good tune, but this rarely happens. If the sight pin ends up well outside the center of the bow, this usually indicates a very weak arrow (or a very stiff spring tension on the cushion plunger) or a clothing or chest clearance problem. When the sight pin is well inside the sight window and is difficult to see (because the sight window is in the way), this is usually the result of a stiff arrow (or a very weak spring tension setting on the cushion plunger).

Setting the Cushion Plunger

Nearly every advanced archer uses a cushion plunger. If you don't use a cushion plunger, your tuning adjustments will be far more limited in the fine-tuning process. To start, set the spring tension at what you would consider a medium pressure by following the manufacturer's instructions. This will probably change later in the tuning process.

Setting Initial Brace Height

Start with the brace height at the lower end of the manufacturer's recommendation or use table 7.1. To locate the optimum brace height for your particular bow, "twist up" the bowstring to make it shorter. This raises the brace height. Note here that raising the brace height also increases bow weight. A very rough estimate of the increase in bow weight would be about 2.5 ounces of additional weight per each 1/4 inch (6 millimeters) of brace height increase. This is important to know because it will have some effect on the tune.

TABLE 7.1   BRACE HEIGHT CHART

Bow length	Brace height range
64 in.	8 1/8-8 3/8 in. (21.0-21.6 cm)
66 in.	8 1/4 -8 1/2 in. (21.3-21.9 cm)
68 in.	8 3/8-8 5/8 in. (21.6-22.2 cm)
70 in.	8 1/2-8 3/4 in. (21.7-22.5 cm)

The brace height, nock-to-string tension, and physical weight of the string determine the specific point at which the arrow separates from the bowstring and the amount of bend the arrow has when the separation occurs. The best brace height for your recurve is one that allows the most compatible launch position for the arrow at the end of the bow's "power stroke." Changing the brace height to a slightly higher or lower position can greatly improve arrow flight and grouping.

Adjusting the Tiller

The term *tiller* refers to the difference in draw weight between the top and bottom limbs. Because we draw the bow with our fingers *above* the center of the string, the fingers of the draw hand are closer to the top limb than to the bottom limb. This causes the top limb to be drawn farther. We set "tiller" as a compensation for this imbalance by making the bottom limb slightly stronger. To adjust the tiller, we set the distance from the top of the riser to the bowstring at 90 degrees to be greater than the distance from the bottom of the riser to the string (again at 90 degrees). The amount of tiller will vary slightly from archer to archer because of the many variations among individuals. As a general rule, the shorter your draw length, the less tiller is required.

A few things that can affect the tiller setting are draw length, drawing hand finger pressure, having a low rather than a medium or high grip, and the design of the bow. As a rough starting point, set the tiller (bottom limb distance to the string slightly shorter than the distance from the string to the top limb) about 1/16 inch for draw lengths up to 26 inches. For draw lengths 26 to 28 inches, set the tiller at 1/8 inch; for draw lengths 28 to 30 inches, set the tiller at 3/16 inch; and for draw lengths over 30 inches, set the draw length at 1/4 inch. Again, these are only starting points.

To assess tiller during your shooting process, be aware of what your sight pattern is doing. When the tiller is set correctly, the sight pin will easily stay on the center of the target through a full draw cycle without the tendency for the sight to move just as you are coming through the clicker. If your sight is bouncing up and down as you are attempting to come through the clicker, the tiller setting is probably not correct. Make very small adjustments to tiller (less than 1/16 inch at a time) and see whether your sight pattern stabilizes. Another indication that the tiller is correct is that you will feel the bow pressing into your bow hand in one concentrated point rather than as a slight rocking feeling in the hand.

Checking Nock-to-Bowstring Tension

The nock tension ("snap fit") necessary to separate the nock from the bowstring serving cleanly can be very critical, especially on light draw weight bows (30 pounds and under). Nock tension should be tight enough that an arrow can easily support its own weight when the arrow is hanging vertically down from the bowstring (nock against the nocking point). To check this, hang your arrow vertically from the bowstring and give the string a sharp tap with your finger on the serving about 1 to 2 inches (2.5 to 5 centimeters) from the arrow nock. The arrow should separate from the string. If it does not, the nock is probably too tight. Choose another nock (they are available in several string groove widths). You can also make the center serving larger or smaller in diameter by choosing different serving thread diameters. If the string tension is too loose, the nock is in danger of slipping off the string at full draw and causing a dry fire. This not only can damage the bow but also can cause a serious bruise to your bow arm.

Setting Up the Arrow Rest

The arrow rest support arm position is critical to achieving good arrow clearance. Some flipper-type rests have an adjustable arm for the arrow rest for easy adjustment. Regardless of the type, the rest needs to be adjusted so that the center of the arrow is contacting the center of the cushion plunger, and the support arm must be adjusted so that it is not visible past the outside of the arrow shaft when observed from an overhead view (see figure 7.5). The support arm of the rest should be at a slight upward angle.

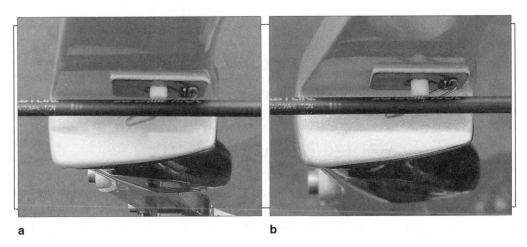

a   b

Figure 7.5 Your rest's support arm must not stick out past the edge of the arrow when viewed from above (a). When set correctly (b) there is less of the rest to interfere with the arrow as it slides along the rest during a shot.

Clicker Warnings

When using a clicker, be sure that the arrow is well supported on the rest and not held in place only by the tension of the clicker. Draw the bow a few times without the clicker to make sure the arrow can be drawn and let down without falling off the arrow rest. The clicker tension and angle are important too. The clicker should not be so stiff that it actually moves the cushion plunger in or places downward pressure on the arrow. To test this, stand in front of a target (just in case you have an unexpected loose of the string) and draw the arrow through the clicker as if you were going to shoot, but do not shoot the arrow.

Rather, watch only the arrow on the rest to detect any movement of the arrow at the moment you pull the arrow through the clicker and the clicker makes contact with the riser. If the arrow moves in any way, either a bounce on the arrow rest or movement due to cushion plunger activation, you need to correct this. There must not be any observable movement of the arrow when the clicker is activated.

Setting the Final Brace Height

Once you have performed all of the previous steps, you can shoot well enough to set your final brace height. All bows are different; even bows of the same make and model can have small variations in limb length. Therefore, you must identify a brace height that fits your particular bow and your particular shooting style. Shoot a few arrows at the suggested beginning brace height; then unstring the bow, add three to four twists to the bowstring, and shoot again. Continue this process until the bow feels smoothest and quietest when shooting.

If the bowstring is too short to allow a brace height at the lower setting, use a slightly longer string. If the string is too long to allow a higher brace height (and starts to knot up from too many twists), try a slightly shorter bowstring. Avoid having too many twists in the string or it will act more like a spring than a string. There should be just enough twists to make it look like a nice round cable.

Starting the Tuning Process

Now that you have completed the preliminary setup of your bow and arrows, you are ready to start the tuning process. Two methods of bow tuning are described on the following pages. They are the bare shaft planing test for initial tuning and then group testing for fine-tuning. They are to be done in that order.

Bare Shaft Planing Test

Bare shaft tuning compares the behavior of fletched and unfletched (i.e., "bare") shafts. The idea is to get the bare and fletched shafts to behave similarly so that, in effect, the fletches have fewer arrow flight irregularities to correct.

The procedure for this test is to shoot at least three fletched shafts at a distance of 15 to 20 yards (or meters). Then shoot two or three identically aimed unfletched shafts. Once you get the bare shafts to impact close to the fletched arrows at 20 yards (or meters), move back 25 to 30 yards (or meters) for a truer reading of the tune. Because determining the arrow spine match to the bow is difficult at a close distance, make sure the bare shafts will hit the target before moving back to a greater distance. The real arrow spine compatibility will be evident at a distance of 30 yards or meters. This is an excellent tuning method as well as the best approach to determine if you have selected the correct arrow spine (shaft size) for your bow.

Arrows that do not fly well and do not group tightly are usually affected by one or more of the following problems:

1. They may *porpoise* in flight. This is when the arrow's nock end shows significant up and down movement in flight.
2. They may *fishtail* in flight. This is when the arrow's nock end shows significant left and right movement in flight.
3. They may not clear the bow properly as they leave the bowstring, which causes them to *minnow*. This is when the arrow's nock end shows similar but smaller movements in flight.

Porpoising

Correct for porpoising first. Porpoising occurs if the arrow leaves the bowstring with the nock too high or too low. Here is how to use the bare shaft tuning method to find the correct nocking point location.

If the unfletched shafts impact above the identically aimed fletched shafts, move the nocking point up on the bowstring until both fletched and unfletched shafts strike at the same elevation (see figure 7.6). If the unfletched shafts impact

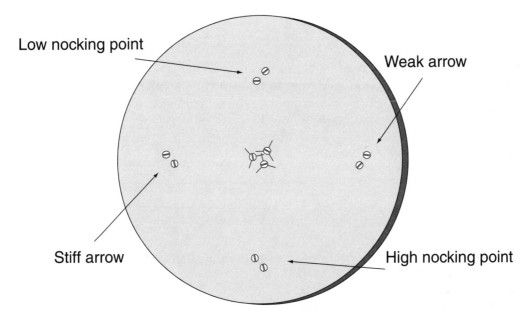

Figure 7.6 The bare shaft planing test. If bare shafts impact high or low compared to the fletched shafts, your arrows will porpoise. Adjust the height of the nocking point indicator to correct this.

below the identically aimed fletched shafts, move the nocking point down on the bowstring slightly and retest. Keep making adjustments until the unfletched shafts hit at the same elevation as the fletched shafts.

It is sometimes desirable to have the bare shaft impact just slightly below the fletched shafts (slightly high nocking point), but the bare shafts must not be more than an inch (2.5 centimeters) below the fletched shafts. Having a nocking point that is too high will often cause very poor grouping at longer distances. This is critical and is a tuning choice more often used for indoor shooting. Conversely, for outdoor competition, it is more often desirable to have the bare shafts impact above the fletched shafts. In this situation, experiment by first having the bare shafts impact slightly above the identically aimed fletched shafts (slightly low nocking point); then move to a longer distance (past 30 meters) and group test. Shoot a few groups; then move your nocking point down farther by 1/32 inch (slightly less than 1 millimeter) at a time to see if grouping improves (this process will be explained in more detail in the fine-tuning section). The nocking point will have more of an effect on grouping than just about any other segment in recurve bow tuning. There are boundaries to consider in the nocking point position as well. If the nocking point is too low, it may force the arrow fletching down into the arrow rest, creating clearance problems. If the nocking point is too high, causing the bare shafts to impact more than a small amount below the fletched shafts, grouping will suffer. Once the preliminary nocking point position is established, the next step is to ensure spine compatibility.

Fishtailing

Fishtailing is usually caused by a mismatched arrow spine. If the arrow leaves the bow with the nock end swinging to one side or the other, fishtailing occurs. The nock end of the arrow will appear to move from side to side as the arrow follows its flight path (see figure 7.7).

Figure 7.7 Fishtailing is the side-to-side oscillation of an arrow in flight. It is similar to porpoising, but porpoising involves up-and-down oscillations.

To use the bare shaft planing test to correct fishtailing, continue to shoot three fletched shafts and two or three identically aimed unfletched shafts. Again, make sure the bare shafts hit the target before moving back farther than 20 yards. If the unfletched shafts impact left of the fletched shafts, as seen in figure 7.6 in the section on porpoising, this means the arrow is too stiff (for a right-handed archer; too weak for a left-handed archer). If the bare shafts impact more than 2 to 3 inches (5 to 8 centimeters) at 20 yards, this means that the bare shafts will be well away from the fletched shafts at a longer distance such as 30 meters, and may not even hit the target.

Clearance

Proper clearance is absolutely essential for optimum grouping consistency and accuracy. This is especially true with ultralightweight arrows such as the Easton A/C/E®, A/C/C®, and A/C/C HyperSpeed® shafts as well as other all-carbon shafts. After you have performed the bare shaft planing test, it is a good idea to check for adequate clearance. To check for clearance, apply dry powder foot spray, dry deodorant spray, or a similar product to the last quarter of the arrow shaft, fletching, arrow rest assembly, and sight window near the arrow rest. Do not disturb the powder sprayed on the arrow and bow while preparing to shoot. The arrow should be shot into a firm target so that it will not penetrate to the powder area. Any contact between the arrow and the bow will leave a trace in the powder on the bow and arrow.

If the arrow fletching and bow make contact, you cannot achieve optimum grouping. By examining the areas where the dry powder spray is scraped off, you can determine the nature of any interference and identify the position of the fletching as the arrow leaves the bow. If there is a clearance problem, you can usually see it in the arrow's flight to the target. A term used to explain the visual flight disturbance is *minnowing*. Minnowing looks much like fishtailing except that the tail of the arrow appears to move from side to side more quickly, and the amount of side swing is usually much less than in fishtailing (see figure 7.8).

Figure 7.8 Minnowing is much like fishtailing except that the oscillations are much smaller and more rapid.

Minnowing indicates inadequate clearance and is caused by the rear portion of the arrow (usually the fletching) contacting the arrow rest or cushion plunger. The following procedures can help you correct clearance problems that cause minnowing:

1. If the arrow fletching is hitting the arrow rest, try rotating your arrow nock 1/32 of a turn. Continue rotating the nock in 1/32-turn increments until you achieve clearance.

2. Make sure your arrow rest support arm does not protrude past the outside of the arrow shaft when viewed from above the arrow.

3. Choose a lower-profile fletching.

4. Make sure your bow hand is well relaxed to eliminate bow hand torque.

5. Move the cushion plunger or rest slightly out from the bow to help increase clearance if the other tuning modifications have no effect.

Group Testing

You may have heard people say that if your arrows group well at 20 yards, they will group at any distance, or if your arrows group at long distances, they will group at short distances. Neither statement is true. There may be a minute mal-adjustment in the equipment that causes poor arrow grouping at one distance but not at the other. What follows here is information that will help you perform the fine-tuning adjustments necessary to eliminate most or all of these minute tuning problems. Following this will be the fine-tuning procedure based on "reading" your arrow groups.

Many archers have experienced poor arrow flight and good grouping or good arrow flight and poor grouping. Poor arrow flight and good grouping is commonly the result of a stiff arrow. The arrow yaws slightly as it leaves the bow, but usually recovers quickly and often produces very acceptable grouping. Although good arrow flight and poor grouping seems contradictory, the phenomenon is somewhat common and relates to the tuning method used, or a lack of fine-tuning. Having perfect arrow flight, or having the bare shafts impact exactly with the fletched shafts using the bare shaft planing test, does not always mean that your arrows will group well; it only means that your arrows fly well. The section on fine-tuning will assist you in obtaining optimal grouping from your equipment as well as good arrow flight.

Arrow grouping patterns often reveal probable arrow flight problems. Two of the most common grouping indicators for determining arrow flight problems are excessive drag and insufficient clearance.

Excessive Drag

Arrows with fletches that are too large or fletches that are offset too far will experience excessive drag, and grouping will often suffer at long distance. For example, if shooting FITA distances, you may experience good grouping on all distances except the longest distance. If this is the case, the arrow likely has too much drag. Excessive drag will cause the arrow to become unstable and more vulnerable to wind drift because of the rapid decay of its forward velocity. It is very important to reduce the drag of lightweight arrows to a minimum to maintain maximum downrange velocity. This can be done by reducing the size (height, length, or both) of the fletching, by reducing the angle of the fletching, or both.

Insufficient Clearance

A clearance problem will usually have the opposite effect of excessive drag. Most often arrow grouping is acceptable at longer distances; however, the shorter-distance groups are not reduced in size proportionate to those at the longer distances. This situation commonly results in short-distance scores that are significantly less than what the longer-distance scores would indicate. If this is a familiar scenario, look for a clearance problem or microdisturbance within the bow and arrow system. To correct it, refer back to the section on clearance on page 112.

Adjusting Arrow Spine

If your arrows are too stiff or too weak, any decrease in the spring tension on the cushion plunger will not likely be of much help. You would be better off using a more effective *gross adjustment* or a combination of adjustments before working with the cushion plunger.

If your arrows seem stiff and your bow weight is adjustable, increase bow weight by approximately one pound. An adjustment of more than one pound is not recommended unless you are in very good physical condition, and even then you should never increase more than two pounds at a time because it could have detrimental effects on your shooting technique and possibly cause an injury. Other gross adjustments that will improve the spine compatibility of an arrow that is too stiff are an increase in arrow point weight and a reduction in the number of strands in the string (reducing the physical weight of the bowstring). Similarly, a decrease in the weight of the center serving material or a decrease in the length of the center serving will have a similar effect, as would a reduction in the weight of the nocking point (e.g., changing from a metal nocking point to a tie-on type).

If the unfletched shafts impact right (weak) of the identically aimed fletched shafts (for a right-handed archer, opposite for a left-handed archer), decrease bow weight slightly, decrease arrow point weight, or both. Here, the bow weight would be the best adjustment to move the bare shafts into or near the same group as the fletched shafts. Going down in bow weight is not a problem other than losing a little arrow speed. Your equipment is basically tuned when the bare shafts and fletched shafts impact at the same or very near the same location.

A well-tuned bow will commonly have the bare shafts impact in a different location from the fletched shafts. Usually, a good tune will have the bare shafts impacting close to the fletched shafts in the horizontal plane, but the nocking point height may be slightly high (bare shaft impacting slightly low of the fletched shafts), or the bare shafts impacting high, by as little or as much as several inches high (low nocking point).

If, after completing this test, the bare shaft impact is more than 3 inches (8 centimeters) to the right (weak) or left (stiff) of the fletched shafts at 20 yards (18 meters), you will most likely need to change shaft size. However, before going to this more costly investment, make sure you are not having a false tuning indicator caused by a clearance problem. Incompatible arrow spine is usually the biggest cause of a clearance problem, but not always. For more information on the adjustments available to the equipment to achieve a better tune, see the clearance section on page 112 and use the suggestions on how to better match the arrow to your bow in the following section.

Adjusting the Bow

Here is a summary of the modifications to your equipment you can make to achieve a better tune.

Bow Weight

Virtually all target-quality recurve bows have an adjustable draw weight system. Bow weight adjustment should be the first tuning consideration if your arrow reaction is significantly stiff or weak. It is important not to increase bow weight more than one to two pounds because doing so could have a detrimental effect on shooting technique. Here is a test to determine if you can physically handle any increase in bow weight. Simply draw and hold your bow at full draw for 60 seconds. If it you can hold the new weight for an entire minute, you can handle the one- to two-pound increase.

Bowstring Weight

Bowstring weight can have a significant effect on arrow spine. Increasing or decreasing the number of strands in the bowstring can influence the arrow's dynamic spine enough to require a shaft size change of up to one full size weaker or stiffer. If your arrow reaction is too stiff, decrease the number of strands in your bowstring. If your arrow reaction is too weak, increase the number of strands. Serving weight (center serving) can also produce the same effect. For example, monofilament center serving will cause the arrow to react stiffer than lighter weight nylon center serving. Simply changing from a metal nocking point to a tie-on nocking point can have a noticeable effect on arrow spine as well because of the weight difference between the two styles of nocking points.

Point or Insert Weight

The arrow's dynamic spine can be tuned by using various point or insert/outsert weight combinations. If your arrow is too weak, go to a lighter insert or point. If your arrow is too stiff, try a heavier insert or point. Continue to change insert or point weights within an acceptable balance point range (9 to 16 percent front of center).

Brace Height

For recurve bows, another way of altering dynamic arrow spine slightly is with brace height. Increasing brace height will make the arrow appear weaker, and decreasing brace height will make the arrow appear stiffer. The reason is, your bow weight actually changes when increasing or decreasing bow weight. However, it is better to establish and set the correct brace height for your bow and use the other tuning variables to create well-tuned equipment. Brace height adjustments are most useful for fine grouping refinement.

Documenting Changes

Once you have completed the bare shaft planing test and before starting the fine-tuning process, write down the exact measurements of your bow in a small booklet you can keep in your quiver. Having all of the equipment information documented will allow you to return to the initial settings if something strange happens during the fine-tuning process. When your bow and arrow are fully compatible and you have achieved optimum arrow flight and grouping, then you will want to redocument the equipment for future reference. Consider this also to be an insurance policy for when something disastrous happens, such as your bowstring breaking the day before a competition. You may be able to get back to a reasonable point quickly with the recorded information. The following information should be included in the documentation:

a. Nocking point height
b. Brace height
c. Tiller
d. Number of strands in the bowstring and type of material
e. Type of center serving and end serving
f. Bowstring weight (use a grain scale)
g. Weight of bow at full draw weight
h. Type of stabilizers used, length, amount of weight on each rod, etc.

Fine-Tuning Your Groups

Next, number all of your arrows. This enables you to plot groups and to track the performance of each individual arrow. This process is very important in discovering which arrows group consistently and which do not.

When you are ready to start the fine-tuning process, use a new 40-centimeter target face as the "plotting" target. This will allow you to record each arrow impact and the number of that arrow to determine common impact points for each arrow in the bunch.

1. Prepare to shoot from a fairly long distance that you are most comfortable with (from 40 to 70 yards/meters).
2. Shoot an end or two to warm up before starting the plotting process.
3. After warming up, shoot a group of 6 to 10 fletched arrows.
4. Write down the number of each arrow and the impact point on the sample "plotting" target.
5. Shoot at least two groups before making any adjustments. Make only one adjustment at a time. Use a different colored pen for each adjustment or use another plotting target so the results are not confused.
6. Examine the groups for patterns.

Carefully examine the arrow grouping patterns you plotted. Note the different shapes of the groups and how the adjustments altered the arrow impact and size of the groups. Examine each arrow by its number. Take careful note of any arrows that did not group consistently with the others. Monitor these arrows to see if they are consistently out of the group because you will probably want to mark these shafts so you will know not to use them in competition.

If the groups are more horizontal than vertical, adjust the nocking point 1/32 inch (.8 millimeter) either up or down. Shoot another two groups and plot the arrows in the same manner as described earlier. For future reference, be sure to write down your bow adjustment on each arrow group you plot. Measure the distance between the high and low arrow to determine an average between the groups. This will help you determine whether the high and low arrow impact has improved in the next grouping sequence. If it has improved, make another adjustment of 1/32 inch (.8 millimeter) in the same direction and shoot another two ends. If the high and low arrow impact is better, continue in that direction until you achieve the most consistent group elevation. Obviously, if the vertical impacts are worse, go back to the original setting and make the same adjustment in the opposite direction.

If the groups are more vertical than horizontal, adjust only the cushion plunger spring tension, not the in/out position of the cushion plunger. Make adjustments to the cushion plunger spring tension in 1/8-turn increments only. Shoot two groups and measure the farthest left and right arrows (eliminating arrows where known mistakes were made in the technique). Make the first spring tension adjustment either stiffer or weaker and shoot two more ends. Again, if the group becomes wider, go back to the original setting and make an adjustment of 1/8 turn in the opposite direction. Compare the groups you just shot and determine if they are getting better or worse. If the groups improved, make another adjustment of 1/8 turn in the same direction and shoot another two ends. Continue this process until you have achieved the tightest possible grouping in the horizontal plane at that distance. If the groups do not change, continue following this procedure until the groups improve or become wider. At the point where the groups just start to get wider, go back 1/8 turn to the previous setting and make a small nocking point adjustment.

The fine-tuning process involves a dynamic relationship between the nocking point height and the cushion plunger spring tension; any change to one affects the other. It is important to understand this relationship. By making only one adjustment at a time, you will be able to continually "compress" the up/down and left/right grouping patterns into the best possible grouping. After completing this procedure, you should find a combination of adjustments that will either slightly or significantly improve arrow grouping.

Once you have completed the long-distance tuning, move to 20 yards (18 meters) and see if the bow continues to group well here too; it should. If not, look for a clearance problem. By shooting all your competition distances at the end of the fine-tuning, you will have confidence in knowing that your equipment can perform well at any distance when shooting competition.

In some instances, you may find an arrow that does not group well with the other arrows in the set. Examine it before you discard it or retire it from competition. Some problems are easily identified; others are not so evident. Shafts that are cracked or dented should be discarded. Some arrows may seem fine, but they may have problems that are not obvious and can cause them to group poorly. Following are common arrow problems that may cause inconsistent or stray impact.

Arrow Straightness. Arrows must be straight for tight grouping. Straightness should be within .004 inch or better for best grouping.

Crooked Nocks. There are several ways to check nock straightness, including commercially available nock gauges and special arrow spinning jigs. Make sure the nocks are absolutely straight. Crooked nocks can cause severe accuracy problems.

Nock Indexing. One nock in the set may be different from the others, which will force the fletching into the arrow rest or cushion plunger when shot. Make sure all nocks are "indexed" the same and that the spacing between the two "clearance fletches" (the two vanes that clear past the arrow rest and cushion plunger) is the same on all arrows in the set. It is not unusual for some fletches to be spaced more closely together than others on the shaft. Always choose the two vanes that are farthest apart to use as the clearance fletches.

Loose or Damaged Fletches. Fletching that is slightly damaged will not usually affect arrow grouping, but if the fletching becomes even slightly detached from the shaft, the arrow will not group with the others or may not even hit the target. In the case of hard plastic vanes, if the rear of any vane is bent, it will also cause a change in impact point.

Loose Points or Inserts. Many archers are not aware of the potential problem of loose points or inserts. Points must be properly installed with good hot melt adhesive or epoxy, depending on the shaft material. Carefully follow the instructions for point or insert installation from the arrow manufacturer. Easton's hot melt adhesive is recommended because other brands are often brittle and may fracture when the arrow impacts hard target butt materials. If the cement fractures or the point is improperly installed, it can result in a separation between the point or insert and the shaft. When separation occurs and the arrow is shot, the separation of the bond between the shaft and point can cause the point to vibrate against the shaft wall, affecting the arrow's natural frequency of vibration and arrow accuracy. To test for point vibration, hold the arrow a few inches below the fletching and lightly tap the point on carpet or grass. If you hear a buzzing sound, the point or insert is probably loose. Heat it and pull it out; then properly reinstall it.

Arrow Weight. Arrow weight is an important consideration for tournament archers and should be checked. Arrows that consistently impact a little high or low of your group may have slight weight variations. A matched set of arrows should have no more than a three-grain spread between the heaviest and lightest arrows in the set. Top tournament archers frequently match their arrows to within one grain or less.

Dancing to a New Tune

In conclusion, don't be afraid to make tuning adjustments; it is the best way to learn how you and your equipment interact. You will learn a lot in the process, and as long as the equipment changes are well documented, you can always go back to any previous settings. When your bow-arrow-archer combination is properly tuned, you won't have any excuses for bad shots or scores—which means you'll get all the credit for the good ones!

8

Tuning Compound Bows and Arrows

Steve Ruis and Claudia Stevenson

Up until about 1950, most Americans shot longbows. After that they shot recurve bows until about 1980, and from then on most Americans shot (shoot!) compound bows. Why the switch to compound bows only a few years after the switch to recurve bows? Because a compound bow can put more energy into an arrow than a bow without its mechanical advantage. It shoots faster and flatter. How does it do this? Most people would answer that it has something to do with the little wheels in the limb tips, but in fact it is because of their much stiffer limbs. Because the limbs are stiffer, the force necessary to draw the bow builds up more quickly than on a noncompound bow (see figure 8.1).

The role of the wheels (eccentrics) is to effect the actual bending of the limbs. (You aren't strong enough.) As each wheel rotates during the draw, it pulls on the *other* limb by means of the buss cable attached to it. When the wheels reach their apex, the pull on the cables actually lessens and so does the drawing force.

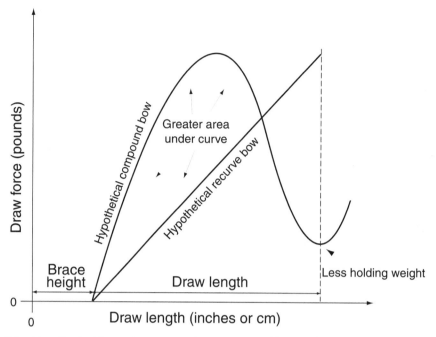

Figure 8.1 Hypothetical force-draw curves for a compound bow and a recurve bow with the same brace heights and peak draw weights. The vertical axis indicates draw force in pounds from 0 upward. The horizontal axis shows how far each bow had been drawn from the rest in inches.

You can see in figure 8.1 why the compound bow is more energetic. The energy stored in the bow is related to the energy under the graph line. The compound bow reaches its peak weight much sooner than does the recurve bow, and even though the curve falls back down as we draw deeper (eventually reaching "the valley" of the force–draw curve), the bow has more energy to give to the arrow. (Cams are designed to raise the draw force even faster and hold it high even longer; therefore, cam bows are faster than similar round wheel bows.) At full draw, the holding weight is a fraction of the peak weight, allowing longer aiming times, a major boon to target shooters.

Compound bows do not automatically make for better shooters. They must be adjusted—tuned—to their shooters to make them most effective, which is the subject of this chapter. A great many archers spend hours and hours tuning their compound bows (and reading about tuning . . . and talking about tuning . . . and worrying about tuning). Some of this is helpful, and some isn't. The catch to understanding tuning is to remember that we can't shoot perfect shots—certainly not 112 of them as in a standard NFAA field round or 144 of them as in a FITA round. Because we are not perfect, we tune our bows and arrows to offset some of our imperfections. The purpose of tuning is to make adjustments in your bow-arrow setup to make your setup more forgiving of less-than-perfect shots.

You can only tune a bow and arrow combination so far without shooting. You can use a shooting machine to tune your arrows, for example. If you shoot all of your arrows from a machine and they don't go into almost the same hole, there is something wrong with the arrows that didn't impact in that hole. But is that arrow the correct arrow for your bow and your release? You can only tell by *you* shooting it. Shooters waste a lot of time trying to tune better than they shoot. If you get nothing else out of this chapter, please remember—*you can only tune as well as you shoot!*

If you are an intermediate shooter, leave the microtuning procedures for later. Get a basic tune and a fine tune, but until you can shoot good groups at substantial distances, you will be wasting your time microtuning. Also, if your form is erratic, tuning won't help. You are much better off practicing shooting than spending appreciable amounts of time trying to tune out irregularities in your shot that are much smaller than your form errors.

There are literally hundreds of tuning schemes. The best one is the one that works best for you. What we present here are some of the tuning methods that have proved successful for thousands of archers—a good place to start.

Before You Tune

There is a short list of things you need to consider before you begin to tune. They have to do with selecting the bow and arrows you will be trying to tune.

Bow Fitting

If your bow doesn't fit you, no amount of tuning will do you any good. Most American archers have their bows set at too long of a draw and draw too much weight for consistent accuracy. If you are an archer who is predominately a bow hunter and you've decided to stay in shape by doing a little target shooting, don't try shooting a 70- or 80-pound hunting bow for targets. Taking a few shots every day of a hunting trip is fine, but drawing a 70-pound bow over a hundred times in one day leads to substantial fatigue and misses. Turn the bow down for target shooting.

Get your draw weight and draw length set correctly first; otherwise you're just wasting your time. With today's lightweight arrows, there is no need to pull a tremendous draw weight. All you need is enough pull to get your arrows where you want them to go comfortably. Getting them there fast is not necessarily an advantage. If you shoot targets at unmarked distances, high arrow speed is an advantage. Speed is also an advantage when shooting in the wind (but not the only one). What makes for high arrow speeds (reflex design riser, low brace height, far from round eccentrics, short axle-to-axle length bows, overdraws) all make for less forgiving bows. But even if speed is desirable, it doesn't require high poundage draw weights. It requires a light, stiff arrow for your bow.

Once you have determined what draw weight is right for you, spend the time to get the draw length right. This may require professional help because correct draw length depends on form, and too many archers determined their draw lengths when their form wasn't good—that is, when they were beginners. If you have the draw length of your bow set wrong, you will never be consistently accurate.

The bow's "grip" also has to be fitted to you (not you to it). Many of the standard grips are too fat to fit your hand properly. (If so, you can grind them down.) Many pros take the grip off and shoot with their bow hand on the riser. The last thing you touch during a shot is the grip. If it isn't right, you will be pushing the bow in ways that will result in erratic arrow flight. This is the part of bow fitting that gives archers the most trouble.

Arrow Fitting

If your arrows are not matched to your bow, they will never tune. To select good arrows, you need to know your correct draw length and draw weight. Again, if these aren't right . . .

There are so many arrow manufacturers, each having many different sizes and combinations, that no specific guidance can be given here other than to find an archery retailer or coach you can trust to serve you well. Following are the variables that affect how the arrows you select actually behave.

- **Arrow Spine.** This corresponds, to some extent, to the stiffness of the arrow. Arrows with incorrect spines are almost impossible to tune. Keep in mind that arrow spine is a much more important variable if you shoot with your fingers and is less important if you shoot with a release aid. In other words, release shooters have a wider range of choices of arrows than do fingers shooters.

- **Arrow Material.** Another variable is the material the arrow is made from (wood, aluminum, carbon). Wood is inconsistent because of its grain. Carbon fiber matrix, the stuff carbon arrows are made of, is inherently stiffer and lighter than aluminum, which is naturally stiffer than wood. Arrows have been made out of literally dozens and dozens of materials (fiberglass, steel, reeds, plastic); what we have today are made of the very best materials.

- **Arrow Mass.** Heavier arrows fly more slowly than do lighter ones and are affected less by crosswinds. If distance is not a problem, heavier arrows are also more stable (wobble less, fly in a more predictable arc). This is simply a matter of physics. Since Olympic competition is now dominated by elimination rounds at 70 meters (a longer distance), Easton Archery Products designed their Olympic-quality arrow, the X10®, to be heavier than their previous arrow (the one all the records were set with), the A/C/E. Of course, heavier arrows don't fly as far, so there are always tradeoffs in the design and selection of arrows.

- **Arrow Length.** Yet another variable is the length of the arrow. Shorter arrows, all other things being the same, are stiffer. If you take a twig and break it, take what is left and break it, take what is left . . . it gets harder and harder to break. It also gets harder and harder to bend; that is, it gets stiffer. Arrows are no different. Therefore, arrow stiffness can be "tuned" by adjusting arrow lengths.

- **Arrow Shape.** The characteristic of the spine is also the result of its shape. Most arrows are hollow tubes, which creates the variables of diameter (the wider, the stiffer), wall thickness (the thicker the wall, the stiffer), and the shape (some arrows are cylindrical, and some are barrel shaped—fatter in the middle than at the ends). Barreled shafts tend to be stiffer than cylindrical shafts, all other things being equal.

- **Arrow Point Mass.** The shape of a hunting broadhead has a great deal to do with how the arrow flies. This is not true for target points. Because target point shape varies very little, the mass of the point affects arrow flight most. Heavier points make the arrow slower and behave as if it were less stiff. Hence, arrow stiffness can be "tuned" by adjusting point weight.

- **Back of Arrow Mass.** The mass of the nock, nock insert, and fletches affect the spine of the arrow as well. The heavier the back of the arrow is, the stiffer the arrow behaves (the effect just the opposite of point mass). This is a little counterintuitive. A heavy mass up front leaves the rest of the shaft whipping around behind it (apparently less spine). A heavy mass in the rear makes the back of the arrow harder to move (apparently more spine).

- **Arrow Balance.** For the arrow to fly well, it must have more weight toward the point than toward the nock. Back-weighted arrows tend to tumble and fly backward. The common measure of this balance is called front of center (FOC). This value is listed as the percent of the distance the balance point of the arrow is in front of the midpoint of the arrow. The FOC of an arrow is not a critical measurement unless you are shooting large numbers of arrows at longer distances (over 50 yards or meters). FITA style shooters trying to shoot groups at 90 meters (98.4 yards) need arrows with fairly high FOC (10 to 15 percent).

- **Fletches.** The size, shape, positions, and material of fletches all have some effect on arrow flight. The purpose of the fletches is to stabilize the flight of the arrow. They do this by "wind resistance" or aerodynamic drag. The fletches, in effect, slow the back part of the arrow, which, because the back part is connected to the front part, causes the back part to *line up* with the front part and *voila*, you have a clean flying arrow. Too much drag and you have a slow arrow. Too little and your arrow wobbles in flight.

Now, here's the scary part. All of these arrow variables are interrelated. Change one, and it changes the effects of the others! So, if one of the following tuning tests suggests that your arrows are too weak (not stiff enough), one option would be to cut them shorter to make them stiffer—but that changes the mass of the arrows and the FOC. Another way to stiffen the arrows would be to use a lighter weight point—but that changes the mass of the arrows and the FOC. You could also lower the draw weight of the bow to get a match. This is done simply by turning the limb bolts on each limb the same amount. Loosening them lowers the draw weight; tightening increases it. This is one of the easiest ways to match an arrow's spine to a bow. If you have to make a large draw weight change, though, you probably have the wrong arrows.

The situation is not entirely hopeless. Most arrow manufacturers supply charts (based on draw pull and arrow length) to help you select their arrows. If you are a novice, stick with less expensive arrows. I once saw a set of Easton X10 arrows, which are possibly the most expensive arrows ever made (they retail for about $350 per dozen *without* points!), for sale at a small fraction of their cost because they were cut too short!

Basic Bow Setup

Assuming that your bow fits you correctly and your arrows fit the bow and you, you still need to make some basic setting adjustments before you can even begin tuning. These need to be done in about the following order because changing one can affect the others.

Setting Tiller

Most modern compound bows are made to be shot at even tiller (see figure 8.2). The only reason to change tiller is to change the feel of the bow in your hand (and we think it is easier to change the grip than the tiller). All such changes involve *only* a fraction of a turn on the limb bolts. When you set your bow's draw weight, turn the limb bolts all the way in and then back both out the same number of turns to get to your draw pull. You should be near even tiller at

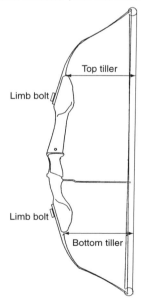

Figure 8.2 Tiller is measured by measuring the distance from the top and bottom of the riser perpendicular to the string (except on cam bows). Most compound bows shoot best with both tiller measurements being about the same (even tiller).

that point. Sometimes an additional quarter or half turn on one bolt is necessary to get to even tiller.

Setting Wheel or Cam Rollover

This applies only to two-wheel or two-cam bows. If you have a two-wheel or two-cam bow, the wheels must be synchronized. With the bow at full draw, check to see if the bowstring comes off the wheels at the same point on both wheels. If this is so (it doesn't have to be perfect), mark the wheels so you can tell later if they somehow get out of synchronization (a rare occurrence). This can be done by making a mark in indelible ink where the wheel aligns to the limb (at rest)—anywhere where you can tell if the marks have moved (see figure 8.3).

Figure 8.3 Place a mark on your wheels next to the edge of a limb. If anything affecting draw length or tiller changes, you will see that the mark has moved

If the wheels are out of synch, get your local bow mechanic to get them in synch for you. If they are just a little out of synch, the bottom wheel should finish last. This keeps the arrow in contact with the arrow rest longer.

Setting a Nocking Point

Setting the nocking point differs depending on whether you use fingers or a release. The best starting point for a release shooter is with the arrow making a right angle with the bowstring. Therefore, the nocking point should be a small distance above "square." You will need a bow square to set this point. If you intend to fine-tune this setting, start with 3/16 to 1/4 inch above a square setting using a bow square, and the arrow itself will be at about 90 degrees. If you shoot with fingers, you want a higher setting, about 3/8 inch above square to start with.

Setting Up Your Arrow Rest

If your arrow rest is set too far from the center of the bow, you will get erratic arrow flight. If it is set too close to the bow's riser, you will also get erratic arrow flight and may have severe problems with the arrow clearing the rest, the bow, or both. To determine where the "just right" line is on your bow, called the centershot, hold a small card between the wheel and the underside (belly) of the bow limb. Mark the edges of the limb and the inner and outer edges of the cam or wheel on the card. Move the card down near the limb pocket (where the limb fits into the riser or handle). Using the outer marks to center the card (the limb is often wider here than at the tip), transfer the position of the wheel or cam onto the limb with light pencil marks. Many people like to use tape so as not to mar the limb. Do this for both limbs. Beiter makes a pair of clips that fit onto bow limbs at their bases to simplify this process.

Nock an arrow and hold the bow out away from you and sight along the bowstring while aligning the string to the marks you just made on the limbs. If you shoot a release, your arrow should be directly behind the string from this view. Since your arrow is attached to the string, the rear end of the arrow is okay. If the tip of the arrow sticks out away from the bow, your rest needs to be moved closer into the bow. If the tip sticks inward, toward the bow, you need to move the rest out. If you shoot with your fingers, your arrow tip should be just visible sticking out away from the bow from behind the string from this view. If it is not, adjust the rest inward or outward accordingly (see figure 8.4).

Measure the distance from the inside surface of the riser to the center of the arrow and record this number. If you fine-tune or even microtune your centershot setting, you will want to record that measurement so you can reset your centershot if your rest breaks or comes loose during a tournament.

Setting Rest Pressure

If you use a launcher rest, the rest only needs as much tension as will keep the rest from sagging with an arrow on it. Higher tension than that can be detrimental to good arrow flight. If you use a plunger-style rest, start in the middle of the stiffness range and use the French or "step back" fine-tuning method or bare shaft testing (finger shooters) to adjust the spring tension.

Setting Peep Height or Kisser Button

The height of your peep sight determines your anchor position to some extent. The easiest way to set this is to install the peep sight in the string, but don't tie it in yet. (Warning: Don't shoot a bow without first tying in the peep sight because the peep can come out during a shot!) With your eyes closed, draw your bow and settle into your most comfortable anchor. Then open your sighting eye. If the peep isn't exactly in front of your eye, move it until it is. (Having a friend help makes this easy.)

Then, set your sight for the distance you want to shoot with your most comfortable anchor. Indoors, this is at the exact distance you will be shooting. Outdoors, some archers set this at the midpoint of the range of distances they will be shooting. For field tournaments, Terry Ragsdale sets his peep at 60 yards! He thinks that a less-than-perfect anchor at 20 yards won't keep him out of the center of

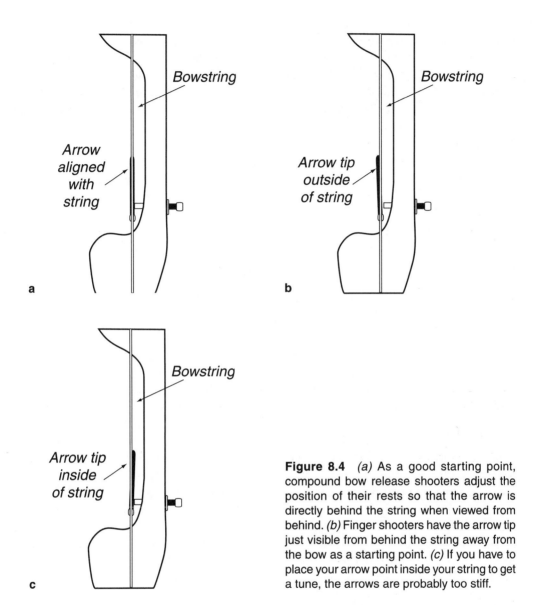

Figure 8.4 *(a)* As a good starting point, compound bow release shooters adjust the position of their rests so that the arrow is directly behind the string when viewed from behind. *(b)* Finger shooters have the arrow tip just visible from behind the string away from the bow as a starting point. *(c)* If you have to place your arrow point inside your string to get a tune, the arrows are probably too stiff.

the target. Tournaments are often won on the longer shots, however, so why not have everything perfect for those. Obviously, this would be way too far for a 3-D shoot, but I think you get the idea.

After setting your sight for the distance you choose, repeat the procedure of drawing with your eyes closed, anchoring, and opening your sighting eye, moving the peep each time until it is perfectly in front of your sighting eye when you open it. Then tie it in place so it doesn't move.

Measure the distance from the bottom of your nocking point to the hole of the peep and *write it down*. We've had plastic peeps break and then found that the spare we carried was a different brand. That's why we measure to the hole in the peep and not some other part of it. You can easily reset it—if you have this measurement. Some coaches recommend that you have a separate bow square for each bow you shoot and write all of these measurements on a piece of tape on the back side of the square. Then if you have that bow square in your quiver, you have all of the vital measurements (and the measuring tool) you need to recover from an equipment failure.

The same procedure works for setting a kisser button, but do not use both a peep sight and a kisser button. The spacing between them changes with the distance you are shooting, and the best you will get is very mixed messages.

Setting Peep Rollover

Nothing is more irritating than a peep sight that doesn't roll over in front of your eye correctly. Some bowstrings don't twist when the bow is drawn, but they are rare. Most strings do twist somewhat when drawn (especially if you shoot with fingers), and the peep must be aligned so you can see through it when at full draw. The best way to do this is to move the peep to a new position between the strands so that it rolls over correctly. (This requires a bow press.)

Some archers prefer to use a peep that incorporates a piece of rubber tubing that attaches to your bow limb or elsewhere and pulls the peep into alignment every time. These work well when newly set up, but invariably the tubing gets old and breaks off near the end. Since there is plenty of slack, you may think you can just reattach the shortened tube and you are back in business. This works somewhat, but after the second or third shortening, the tubing is too short and distorts the position of the string at full draw, which *moves your peep sight to a different position* and you start missing unexpectedly. I don't recommend these peep aligners.

Set your peep up right (it may take two or three tries) and it will roll over correctly for you for the life of the string. If it doesn't, something is wrong (broken strand in the bowstring, stretched string or cable).

Choosing Peep Sight Size

The size of the hole in the peep sight is determined by your own vision and the amount of light available. For shooting in the woods or an indoor tournament, where the amount of light is low, you will want to use a larger peep, which lets in more light to your eye. Outside in bright sunlight you may want to use a smaller one. Target shooters always want a large enough peep so they can see the body of their scope to make sure it is exactly centered in the peep each time.

Setting Other Components

The type and style of stabilizer you use can affect where your arrows hit on the target. Whatever size or type of stabilizer you use, you want the bow to be balanced in your hand after the shot or you want the top limb to roll forward *slowly*. Longer stabilizers will make the bow roll over faster, as will putting more weight on the tip of the stabilizer. If you like a long stabilizer or one with a fair amount of weight at its tip, use a back weight on your riser to balance out some of the rollover. A bow that rolls over rapidly may be rolling while the arrow is still on the bow!

A stabilizer is supposed to steady your aim, make the bow harder to move while aiming, and maybe absorb shock. The more mass it adds and the farther it is from the bow, the more the bow resists moving. This is critical during the shot. The last thing the arrow touches is the rest (release shooter). If the bow jumps sideways or torques in your hand because of improperly balanced stabilizers, you are going to drop points you shouldn't. Have someone (with good eyes) watch you shoot, or better, videotape yourself and watch what happens to your bow as the shot is loosed. The stabilizer (and everything attached to it) should move straight toward the target when the shot is loosed. (Then it will swing to the side because the "slack" in your bow arm is taken up, but this is after the arrow is gone.) If the bow "kicks" in any other direction, check your bow's stabilizers for balance.

Make sure your bow is also a good shock absorber. Only about 75 percent of the energy you put into the bow when you draw it gets transferred to the arrow during the shot. The rest of the energy has to go somewhere, and the only other thing in contact with the bow is you! The accumulated shock to your bow arm from a long day's shooting can cause you to shake in the latter part of the day. Good shock absorbing stabilizers can protect you from this wear and tear. If your stabilizer doesn't absorb shock, or enough of the shock, there are a great many shock absorbing doodads you can put on your bow. They are well worth the money.

Miscellaneous Components

The following are not parts of the bow-arrow system, but if they aren't right, they will cause you problems that will prevent you from getting a forgiving bow setup.

Bow Slings. You must use a bow sling to shoot well consistently. Setting it is simple, but many people set them too loose or too tight. Too tight and they will cause the bow to react to movements in your arm. Too loose and you may not trust them to do their job and you will end up grabbing the bow after each shot. You know the pattern without thinking about it: you *shoot-grab, shoot-grab, shoot-grab, then grab-shoot!* Another miss and you may not even know why. Your sling should be snug on your wrist or in your hand; it needs to allow some *slack*, but just a little.

Armguards. If the string slaps your wrist, your mind will start doing all kinds of weird things to avoid the pain. If you need an armguard, wear one—don't be macho. Compound bow shooters who regularly hit their wrists are having form problems (typically from having too long of a draw).

Bow Tuning Procedures

Whew! Getting a bow ready to tune takes a lot of work. If any part of your basic bow setup is "off," it will distort your form and prevent the tuning procedures from showing anything but the inconsistencies in your form. Don't skip any of these.

Fine-tuning consists of adjustments you can make in the nocking point height and centershot position of your rest, in that order. Everything from this point onward assumes that you have a good basic bow setup.

Fine-Tuning Nocking Point Height

One way to fine-tune this setting is to put a one-inch-wide piece of tape horizontally on a piece of cardboard as a target. Shoot a small set of arrows at this tape from 15 to 20 yards or meters. Don't worry about where the arrows go left and right; just space them out so you don't damage your arrows. Record the height of the group and disregard any obvious bad shots. Move your nocking point a small increment (1/32 inch) up or down from the starting position and shoot another group. Measure the height of this group. If the group is less high, this may be a better nocking point setting. Keep making small adjustments in the same direction until the group gets taller. The setting that gives you the narrowest group is the best setting. If you started moving the nocking point up, go back to your original setting (You did write down the original setting, didn't you?) and try moving it down, again in small increments. Obviously, if you can't hold a small group, your form may not yet be up to this method of fine-tuning your nocking point, or you may just be shooting from too far away.

Another way for fingers shooters to fine-tune their nocking point setting is with *bare shaft testing* (see page 134). Be sure to record the best setting. Also, changing arrow sizes changes all of this and requires you to reset your nocking point.

Fine-Tuning Centershot

Once you have tuned your bow fairly well, you can fine-tune your centershot setting. Get out the one-inch tape again, but this time put a strip vertically on a piece of cardboard. Shoot a small set of arrows at this tape from 15 to 20 yards or meters. Don't worry about where the arrows go up and down; just space them out so you don't damage them. Record the width of the group and disregard any obvious bad shots. Move your rest a very small increment in or out from the starting position and shoot another group. Measure the width of the group. If it is tighter (not as wide), this may be a better centershot setting. Keep making small adjustments in the same direction until the group gets wider. The setting that gives you the narrowest group is the best setting. If you started moving the rest away from the riser, go back to your original setting and try closer and so on. Obviously, if you can't hold a small group, your form may not yet be up to this method of fine-tuning your centershot, or you may just be shooting from too far away. Use your own judgment here, or better, work with a coach.

Another method of fine-tuning centershot is the French or "walk back" method. Find a tall target butt and place a small target very near the top of it. Stand about 10 yards from the butt, set your sight for 10 yards, and shoot one arrow (or a group of three if you are a perfectionist). Move back five yards and, without resetting your sight, shoot another arrow (or set). (Warning: These may actually go higher than the first, so allow room for this.) Keep moving back in five-yard or other regular increments, shooting arrows at each distance without resetting your sight. Stop before your arrows hit the ground instead of the target.

If your centershot is perfect, the arrows should march down the butt in a straight line. If the arrows form a straight line but are angled to either side, there is a left-right pressure problem with the rest. (For a right-handed archer, if you are using a plunger-type rest, the spring is too weak if the arrows trail off to the right; the reverse is true if you are left-handed.) If the arrow line curves out to the right and comes back toward the center, the rest is too far to the right. If the arrow line curves out to the left and comes back toward the center, the rest is too far to the left. Make very small adjustments to the left-right position of the rest and reshoot.

Paper Testing

Many pro shops have frames that can be used for paper testing. You can also make one out of wood or PVC pipe fairly easily. The idea is to stretch a sheet of paper on the frame and tape or clamp it there. Put the frame several yards in front of a target butt. Stand 4 to 5 yards (release) or 8 to 10 yards (fingers) in front of the paper and shoot arrows through the paper. The hole the arrow makes tells you whether the tail of the arrow is following the tip (see figure 8.5).

The problem with paper tuning is that it can tell you only what is happening at the distance you are standing from the paper. If you stand a different distance from the paper, it may tell you something quite different. Basically, paper

Point

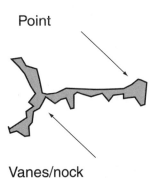

Vanes/nock

Figure 8.5 Shooting through a pane of paper gives a record of the attitude of the arrow as it passes through. The arrow that made this tear was oscillating left and right, as seen from where the point went through the paper and where the vanes went through slightly later.

testing tells you what the back end of the arrow is doing. It is a simple form of testing that will tell you whether your nocking point or centershot is way off and help you get to a good starting position for fine-tuning. Archers who spend hours adjusting their bows to give a perfect "bullet hole" tear are probably wasting their time.

Bare Shaft Testing

Bare shaft testing is for finger shooters. For this kind of testing you need two arrows with no fletches. If you've already fletched them all, you'll need to strip two of them. Ideally, the bare shafts should weigh exactly the same as the fletched ones. You can try adding a weight equivalent to the difference of the fletched and stripped shafts to the back of the bare shafts with shrink tubing or by gluing small lead shot in the hollow space in the nocks.

From about 15 yards set your sight so you can get a good group of three arrows in the center of a target. Then shoot the two bare shafts. (You shoot two to tell if you shot a good shot with the bare shaft; they should group!)

- If the bare shafts strike the target *above* the fletched group, your *nocking point is too low*.

- If the bare shafts strike the target *below* the fletched group, your *nocking point is too high*.

- If the bare shafts strike the target to the *left* of the fletched group, your *rest is too far to the left*.

- If the bare shafts strike the target to the *right* of the fletched group, your *rest is too far to the right*.

- If the bare shafts strike the target anywhere else relative to the fletched group, you have a combination of adjustments to make.

Many top finger shooters actually prefer a slightly low-left impact point for the bare shafts (for right-handed archers; low-right for left-handers). The thought is that the arrow coming out of the bow with the nock slightly high and away from the bow should be more forgiving of a less-than-perfect release.

If you find that you cannot tune out a left or right bare shaft impact point with a left-right adjustment of your sight, try changing the pressure on your plunger button. If you do not have such a setting, or if that doesn't remove the side impact of the bare shafts, check your arrow spine. The spine (see the previous discussion) of the arrow is critical for fingers shooters. If the arrow is too stiff, it will cause bare shafts to hit left of the fletched group. If the arrow is too weak, it will cause bare shafts to hit right of the fletched group. These directions are reversed if you are left-handed. A poor spine match to your bow will result in bigger groups and poorer performance at short distances (the fletches have less time to correct the arrow flight).

Arrow Tuning Procedures

So far our discussion has been about the bow, but it is a bow-arrow system we are tuning here. If you have done all of the preceding and your arrows still wobble visibly while in flight, you may have a clearance problem; that is, the arrow is brushing the rest or bow on its way past. In the following section we will discuss how to correct that.

Powder Testing

A prime cause of erratic arrow flight is the arrow hitting the rest (or the bow!) as it leaves the bow. Arrows hitting the rest or bow on their way are going to behave too erratically to tune. This arrow clearance problem has to be handled first. To check for good arrow clearance, spray the back of an arrow with spray powder (use foot powder or whatever you can find in an aerosol spray can—you can clean them off later), then shoot the arrow into a target stiff enough that the arrow doesn't penetrate and wipe off the powder. Check the arrow for trails in the powder. At most, there should be tracks where the arrow shaft slid along the rest. Also check the rest and the riser for tracks of powder. (You can also spray the riser and rest and look for tracks there.) If the vanes are contacting anything, rotate the arrow's nock a small amount and retest. Align all of the nocks on the other arrows to the arrow that shows good clearance (see Aligning Your Nocks on page 136).

Once you have eliminated any clearance problems, the other problems associated with arrows are generally related with how they group in the target. Here are some tools to deal with grouping problems.

Weighing Your Arrows

Even small differences in weight can cause significant differences in arrow impact at longer ranges. What you want is a set of arrows with very little difference between them. Some people weigh their arrows and then shoot them in sets according to how close they are in weight.

A better way is to weigh the fletched shafts and points of your arrows *separately*. You'll need to number or label your arrows and the points with an indelible marker to tell them apart. (You should always number your arrows so you can tell which arrow is which when an arrow stops grouping with the others—but don't put the number where you can see it. If an arrow is suspect, and you know it, it will distract you when you are shooting it.) Line the arrow points up from heaviest to lightest. Match the lightest shafts with the heaviest points. If the totals are all within one to two grains of each other, you're done!

If they aren't close enough in mass, continue. For aluminum arrows add hot melt glue into the hollow of the point of the lightest arrow until that tip-arrow combination weighs as much as the heaviest combination. Tiny slivers or powdered hot melt glue works best. Warm the point gently to melt that glue into the inside of the point. The last one stays unchanged. Now glue in the tips. For carbon arrows, grind the back of the point of the heaviest combination until that tip-arrow combination weighs as little as the lightest combination. Continue with the rest. The last one stays unchanged. Now glue in the tips. Professional archers match their arrows' weights to within just a few *tenths of a grain*! (1 grain = .00228 ounce).

Aligning Your Nocks

Many archers shoot with nocks that are in different alignments. This variation is a source of misses. Get a nock alignment gauge and align the nocks all to the arrow that gives you the best rest clearance. Then leave them alone.

Spin Testing Your Arrows

Arrow spin testers generally cost less than $30. The best ones allow the arrow to spin quite a few seconds at a relatively high revolution rate. While the arrow is spinning, you can see whether the nocks are symmetrical. (Nocks can be poorly made or be knocked out of alignment when struck by another arrow.) Similarly, you should inspect the arrow points. Arrows can be bent right behind the point, which may not show up with a casual hand spinning of the arrow. If an arrow is bent, it will tend to bounce up and down on the spinner. A spin tester is well worth the money as a "miss prevention tool."

Ensuring Correct Arrow Spine

Arrow spine is critical for fingers shooters, but not as important for release shooters. The best test of whether your arrows are spined correctly for your bow is *group testing*. Over- or underspined arrows will fly and group poorly. When a shot is loosed with a release, the arrow can't move as fast as the string wants it to go, so it flexes. The weaker the arrow, the more it flexes. For release shooters, this flexing is largely up and down with a smaller side-to-side component. For finger shooters, the string comes off the string fingers somewhat sideways, so the flexing is mostly side to side.

When archers shot only wood (i.e., noncentershot) bows, someone noticed that the string was directly behind the limbs and therefore the arrow's nock was directly behind the bow when on the string. The arrow necessarily pointed off to the left (for a right-handed archer). But the arrow did not fly off to the left when shot. Why didn't the arrow shoot off to the left if pointed that way? This is the archer's paradox. The solution came with the advent of high-speed photography (in the 1920s), which showed the arrow bending around the bow! The bending of even the stiffest arrows is noticeable to the high-speed camera. If the arrow flexes back too fast, the rear end of it will hit the bow. If it doesn't flex back fast enough, the arrow will fly erratically to the left. So an arrow spine match must be made to the bow.

When choosing arrows, use a good spine chart to make a selection; then find a buddy who will loan you some arrows to test. When you find ones you can get good groups with, then open your wallet. Otherwise this can get expensive!

Adjusting the Arrows to the Bow

If the arrows are close to the right spine, there are adjustments you can make. If the arrows are a little too stiff, add draw weight to match them (heavier draws require stiffer arrows) and vice versa. You may also have to adjust rest pressures (if of the plunger type). If the bow is right where you want it and you don't want to change anything, you can make the arrows weaker by not cutting them as short or stiffer by cutting them shorter. (Warning: Don't cut them so short that the arrow falls off the rest at the maximum draw length of the bow. This is dangerous!)

Choosing a Fletch

You can also make arrows weaker by using heavier points or lighter fletches. You can make arrows stiffer by using lighter points or heavier fletches. Some people shoot with feathers as fletching; others use vanes. Which should you use? This is somewhat a matter of personal choice, but consider what would happen if you were to switch from vanes to feathers of the same size. Your arrows would now be lighter (feathers are inherently lighter than the same size plastic vane), and hence you would gain arrow speed and cast (out to about 40 yards). The feathers are more fragile, so you would have to take better care of them or replace them more often. Your arrows would now be noisier. The feathers also would not perform as well as vanes when wet. Also, since the feathers weigh less and they are on the back of the arrow, the arrow will behave as if it had a weaker spine (adding weight to the front of an arrow weakens it, to the rear stiffens it). No choice in arrow components is trivial.

Target shooters (release) generally shoot about two-inch fletches outdoors. Indoor target shooters use everything under the sun (because the distances are short), often shooting three- or four-inch feathers or vanes. Bigger vanes correct release flaws more quickly. Hunters prefer about four- to five-inch fletches (big broadheads require more *steerage* from the back of the arrow to fly well). Finger target shooters tend to need somewhat larger fletches. Fingers shooters may prefer feathers largely because of the perception that feathers correct the side-to-side oscillations of the arrow more quickly, but will shoot vanes because they are sturdier. Release shooters prefer vanes because, when shooting tight groups, feathers would get shot to pieces in short order.

Whether you shoot feathers or vanes, you need to put them on the arrows at a slight (1- to 2-degree) angle. Don't fletch them straight (aligned to the shaft). Whether you fletch with a straight clamp or a helical one is pretty much immaterial as long as you angle them. Frank Pearson likes helical fletchings because they are more visible in binoculars or spotting scopes!

For More Information

More has been written about tuning than any other archery subject (possibly because we want to believe it's the bow's fault for poor shooting), so information

Coaching and Being Coached

M.J. Rogers

Unfortunately, most archers get started in archery without the benefit of a coach. Perhaps your "coach" may have been the friend who got you started. In this chapter we will address the question of why you need a coach and even entertain the idea that becoming a coach can be beneficial to you as an archer.

Why Do I Need a Coach?

Archery is different from other sports. If you, as a youngster, were to pursue football, baseball, tennis, golf, swimming, or any other sporting endeavor and decided you wanted to get better, you would seek out a coach. There are youth programs galore in these other sports—Little League, Peewee football, school- and church-related sports programs, 4-H sports programs, and so forth. In archery we have the 4-H shooting sports programs, summer camp archery programs, and the National Archery Association's JOAD (Junior Olympic Archery Development) program. In spite of the existence of these programs and the fact that the major archery associations provide lists of their coaches by phone or on the Internet, most archers are taught by friends. Rather than trying to divine the reasons for this phenomenon, let's explore what you can expect from an archery coach.

The Coach and Athlete Relationship

Because archery is such a technical sport, "drop-in" coaching sessions are rarely effective. Someone hoping to help you improve as an archer must see you over a period of time, see how you react to practice and tournament pressure, and see how you incorporate new knowledge and techniques. This requires a commitment of time and energy from both you and your coach.

The ties you develop with your coach are essential to your advancement in the sport. Any critique (positive or negative) during training is accepted much better when trust exists. Trust is developed when your coach's credentials (successes) are accepted. In most cases, the coach's reputation will suffice as coaching credentials; however, you might not accept at face value a coach's success for this validation or trust. Whatever the case, the relationship grows or founders based on whether you benefit by following the path worked out between the two of you. If you commit to excellence with your attention, time, action, and communication, you should expect to see a positive effect. For example, if upon inspection of your equipment, your coach suggests changes in setup or tune, you should be willing to commit the time to make these changes and test them out. If the result of the changes is better scores, the relationship between you and your coach is strengthened. In archery, the target is the final arbiter. As the

The relationship between coach and archer is quite personal and flourishes or founders based on the degree of trust built into it.

relationship is strengthened, trust grows, and you become more willing to take greater risks to get better. The 2000 Olympic gold medalist, Simon Fairweather, rebuilt his shot from the ground up at the advice of his coach only a year and a half before the Olympic Games. Such daring can only happen when there is absolute trust in that relationship.

A coach's relationship with an archer is often referred to as rapport. The typical coach/athlete relationship is that of older (wiser) person to younger (less experienced) person. You and your coach become a training team. In this team, which may include others (such as your parents if you are a younger archer), age is not an issue; experience and coaching ability defines your coach's effectiveness. The objective of your coach, as a member of the team, is exclusively for the team to attain its goals. Regardless of whether your coach is paid for services, his or her role and responsibility is your success first and foremost. To achieve this, your coach must keep all aspects of the developed trust within the confines of the team. The only exception to this is if a qualified sport psychologist becomes a member of your team.

The training of a coach is often a long and arduous process requiring many hours of tutelage under more experienced coaches. The NAA's coach training program has five levels. Only at Level 3 do coaches become qualified to work with individual archers. The Level 4 coaches are national team-level coaches, and they have four sublevels to work through (4A through 4D). Each level or sublevel requires additional training and experience (and cost!). Coaches need to seek out as much archery knowledge by reading the literature on the development of archery skill and consulting with more experienced coaches and archers as they can. At other times coaches may need to compromise, politick, and work in less than ideal circumstances. Overall, a coach's skill will consist of archery technique knowledge, honesty, communication skills, equipment knowledge, and archery resources.

Your parents or spouse play a major part in your training. These relationships have much deeper, more longstanding ties than any coach could expect to develop. These people are important in your life, spend extended time with you, are more of a mentor figure than your coach, may have goals different from yours, or may have conflicting coaching philosophies. They should not be ignored, but rather should be an integral part of the training plans for the team. Thus, coaches do not work with just archers. They work with the archer's team.

Coaches consider archers to be athletes. Athletes are like all other humans. They respond to positive reinforcement of accomplished performances. When a perceived mentor critiques an athlete, the athlete's natural response is to perform in a manner that solicits more praise and less criticism. Thus, a coach, as a perceived mentor, is an athlete trainer. Archer-athletes use coaches primarily to get better faster and to learn from their experiences. Just as archer-athletes use other training aids, they use coaches to advance their training.

Coaching Competitions

Competitions are the proving ground of the training plans laid out by you and your coach months or maybe years before. Competitions provide opportunities for your team to test its strategies. Provided your communication is good, you and your coach will be able to assist each other in exploiting the competition's opportunities. One of the most difficult realities of competition is scoring. This is the report card for you and your coach. Early in the team development, success or failure is sometimes attributed to only one part of the team, but the competition grades (match play or tournament results) are really a team effort. You and your coach came in the same car, assisted each other with equipment, and observed at the same target assignment; you were a team, and as such you both accepted the responsibility for the grades from the event. Competitions are learning experiences.

When evaluating a competition, your coach can help you by asking questions such as the following:

- Was the tournament plan a success?
- What part of the training needs improvement?
- When did the plan fail?
- How do we repeat this success?

You and your coach should ask and answer these questions at training sessions following each competition. You should then talk about what improvements are necessary for the next goal. The challenge is to learn from failures and progress toward a better outcome at the next event. This is the cycle of competition and practice. At practice you and your coach look at all of the components of the event (shooting, scoring, evaluation, and corrections), and then address the components that need work. This is how archery performances are enhanced. Competitions are where practice is tested. Scores are written, good or bad grades, no second chances. You and your coach, as a team, should use mistakes for the improvement of your next performance.

Your team is looking for successes as well as failures. Success is the reward for a job well done and should not be overlooked. It is easy for your coach or you to be too critical of a performance. A novice's success is when event scores are within 10 percent of practice scores. Your coach is the lead for event evaluation. This is the team—the coach coaches; you shoot. The end product of the team's effort is getting closer to your goals at competition.

Coaching Practices

Practice is where your team assembles the systems that will provide the best opportunity for success at competition. Practice is your evaluation time; proficiency is your goal. Practice provides the venue for experimentation with techniques and equipment. It is a planned time for evaluations, then for corrections or reinforcement.

Framework for Development

The shot sequence developed through either individual or coached training is unique to each archer. Few are able to establish a textbook shot routine or need to, but your routine is what your team has to work with. Whatever the sequence, it needs to be written down. This not only reinforces the sequence but also establishes specificity to the parts. Asking you for descriptive words for the steps in your shot sequence provides your coach with key words for each component of the sequence. Each key word can help you focus when part of the sequence breaks down in competition, either at your coach's prompting or your own.

Soon after you begin shooting, you develop the "feel" of your shot. Good or bad, this becomes "your" shot. Your coach can teach you to sense how closely each shot compares to the last one. Your body then learns what your trained or habitual shot feels like. This is your form of personal instant replay. During practice sessions your coach provides commentary for this instant replay. This helps to ingrain the correct feel to your own shot. Your coach can also help you recognize subtle differences in your sequence so when practicing alone, or during events, you will develop a sense of self-analysis. Practice provides a time to analyze, then test, and then improve your personalized shot sequence.

Working the Plan

Each practice session needs a plan of action. Otherwise you are just shooting arrows without direction. The primary direction for the plan comes from the shot sequence, the part(s) that have not become second nature. Flaws dictate what is in the practice plan. The adage "learn from your mistakes" is very applicable. Your coach's task is to determine what needs the most attention. This becomes the plan so that the team can use the limited training time most effectively.

The plan must also include how to accomplish your goals. This is best when looked at in reverse order. Consider goals that are two, three, or four years out to help determine where to begin. Then incorporate practice measures that indicate that you are making progress and at the correct pace.

Facing Problems

What will you do when _____ happens? Your team must discuss alternatives when problems occur. Often, weather, practice time, equipment, or any number of other problems will throw schedules off. Having a contingency plan makes problems less devastating. Having a plan of action in place when it rains; when practice areas are unavailable; or when the bow, string, rests, release aid, or arrows need fixing takes enormous pressure off your relationship with your coach. Have a plan B, and practice it.

Many problems can't be avoided. As part of goal planning, the team should address family and career, which account for the majority of planning problems. The entire support team, including parents and spouses, should be part of the planning. If the entire team is not involved, the derailment of the long-term goals is imminent. Coaches should be the spearhead for these planning sessions. Their experience should help you and your support team to work through any difficulties.

When The Coach Is Not There

Independence is ultimately what your coach is providing. Archery is an *individual* sport. Whether competing as an individual or as a team member, success is always based on your individual success. Archery doesn't allow for competitors or teammates to block, pass, interfere, or intercept. Each archer must develop self-reliance through individual persistence or with the aid of a coach. Knowing your equipment, competition rules and strategies, and your shot routine are all part of becoming complete in the sport skill. An experienced coach can certainly help you achieve these goals much more quickly.

A coach can see what you cannot and can be a great help, but the goal is always the independence of the archer.

The Master Coaching Plan

Wrap everything into the package of a master plan. This will include all goal setting strategies, career planning, school, family involvement, and more. The question is, What do you want from learning the sport skill? Think of the primary goal as your dream house. All the parts and steps along the way build the house. As you begin to develop and build this house, many things are unknown to you, so you use an architect, carpenter, supplier, mason, plumber, and other craftsmen to achieve your goal. As with any major project, it can and will take years to complete. The coach's involvement depends on your satisfaction level. Some athletes' goals are higher than others. Whereas some are satisfied with recreational involvement, others strive for excellence at the highest levels of competition. Regardless, there is always something to be learned in the sport skill of archery.

So, did this discussion of coaches and archers encourage you to seek out a coach? If so, realize that coaches, like archers, have strengths and weaknesses. Some coaches are very equipment literate but weak in tournament management training. Others are great as mental skills coaches or planners and less good at equipment problem solving. You need to match your needs to the strengths and weaknesses of a coach. Of course, you may need a coach to figure out what you need.

Some elite archers are coached by other elite archers because often the only people who understand what goes on for an elite archer are other elite archers or coaches who have been elite archers. Imagine being coached by someone who has "been there, done that" in archery. Does that make you feel more secure? It should. Experience is the hardest teacher, and experience can be learned from the more experienced.

Becoming a coach to less experienced archers is a good way to pay something back to the sport that gives you so much. It is also a way to learn more about what it might take for you to reach your next level as an archer. If you choose this route, consult the Web sites of the major archery organizations for information on their coach training programs.

10

Dealing With Difficulties

Steve recently was preparing to shoot in a large FITA shoot. His goal was to shoot a personal best score. He had everything covered. All of his gear (bow, backup bow, spotting scope, tools, everything) was packed. All of his practice was done. All of his sight marks were as good as they get. He even had his meals planned and packed. He had a list of people he wanted to connect with at the shoot so he wouldn't forget any of them. He was prepared with a capital P! The morning of the shoot, he got into his car and headed out. Two miles from home a deer sprang in front of his car and wham! He turned around and spent the rest of the weekend calling the insurance company and working on his car.

Sometimes, even if you think you have prepared all that you can, something you didn't expect happens. This chapter will help you prepare for difficulties—in competition and in practice.

Adjusting Your Attitude

When you are experiencing difficulties, how do you react? If you throw a hissy fit every time something goes wrong, you are unlikely to succeed at archery. In other words, your attitude is the most important aspect of dealing with difficulties. If you can view

**Steve Ruis and
Claudia Stevenson**

difficulties as normal or even as just an addition to the challenges you face on a regular basis, you are far more likely to be successful in archery (or even life in general). A good way to have a good attitude toward difficulties is to be prepared for them.

Expecting the Elements

A great many parts of archery are under your control, and some aren't. Often the challenge is not just the target but dealing with the elements.

Rain

You are halfway through a tournament, and it begins to rain. A member of your target group says, "I hate the rain! I always shoot poorly!" You think, *My score will not be as high as it might be because of the rain, but we all have the same handicap, so let's see what I can do!* Who do you think is going to do better? This is an example of having a positive attitude toward a difficulty.

Similarly, if you take careful note of how you shoot in the rain, you may be able to offset some of the negative effects on your score. For example, if your notes from previous performances indicate that you tend to shoot about three inches low at 70 meters during a steady rain, you could try adjusting your

Competitions don't stop if it begins to rain. What will you do? Your attitude and careful preparation will determine how well you do.

sight down. If the rain is light, maybe you need just half of that adjustment. Taking positive action to deal with a difficulty will always bring you more success than fuming over the conditions and just shooting away to get the ordeal over with.

Being prepared also means having appropriate clothing (rain slickers that fit tightly enough, waterproof boots or shoes, etc.), a towel to dry off your equipment, even an umbrella. You may need some paper tissues to dry small items. If you shoot with a scope, bring something to keep it dry or to dry it if it gets wet. We tend to use a lot of baggies. Big baggies can be inverted over the arrows in your quiver to keep them dry, and small ones can be used to keep backup tabs or releases dry.

Wind

If the wind is blowing in gusts, good luck; you will need lots of it to shoot decent scores. If the wind is steady, you have many more options. The most important factor is experience. The more you have to deal with the wind, the better you'll get. Until you get the experience, consider that wind blowing in your face or toward the target is going to affect the impact point up and down.

Winds from the left and right will blow the arrows to hit right and left of the intended target. The simplest technique is to let your arrows tell you where to aim. If, during a wind from behind, your first arrow lands 12 inches high, aim 12 inches low for your next shot (assuming the wind is the same). If the wind is from the left and your arrow hits 8 inches to the right, aim 8 inches to the left. We don't recommend changing your sight windage or elevation because if the wind changes, you probably won't be able to remember all of the sight changes you made.

Studies show that the greatest effect of the wind is on you, not your arrows. The steadier you are, the better you will shoot. Read Annette's archery fitness chapter (chapter 5) and work on building up your leg strength.

Heat and Humidity

You must be prepared for exposure to the sun's rays and the heat and humidity of the competition site. A wide-brimmed hat to keep the sun off and sunblock lotion are necessities. Drink plenty of fluids (avoid sugary drinks, though), and know the signs of heat fatigue.

High humidity slows down your primary cooling system, evaporation of perspiration. In such conditions you must take special care to keep your cool. Personal cooling devices and ice packs kept in coolers and applied to areas where there is a lot of blood flow (such as your neck) will help. Wear clothing that doesn't trap heat and that wicks away perspiration. Read Pedro Serralheiro's fine article (*Archery Focus* 2002) if your shooting venues are hot and humid.

Confronting the Competition

We have found, in general, that dealing with fellow competitors is delightful. Most of these people are personable, friendly, and even helpful when we are struggling. But occasionally you will have "the shooting partner from hell." Most of the time we shrug and think, *What can I do?* and then focus on not letting the disruptive behavior of a fellow competitor interfere with how we are shooting.

You should not ignore a shooting partner who is cheating or is otherwise violating the rules. That is what judges and other shoot officials are for. Don't feel that enforcing shoot rules is an antisocial act. You may find others thanking you for doing something they wanted to do but couldn't.

Some competitors will deliberately try to get "in your kitchen"—that is, act in ways to disrupt your shooting. This is surely not good sporting behavior, but it is something you might encounter. Try to focus on your game, and nothing else. You are in control; you don't have to react to the taunts or ploys of an overcompetitive target partner. After the shoot, make your way to the parking lot and let the air out of his tires. You will feel better. (Just kidding!)

Treating Target Panic

Target panic is probably the most contentious topic in all of archery today. This is not surprising. What is surprising is that this malady has been around for hundreds of years (it has been documented in almost every book about archery in the English language). Until recently, though, little progress has been made in addressing it. What is it? Good question! In an article entitled "It" in the early 1960s, Milan Elott wrote, "We call it 'It' because it has no proper name, and 'It' takes many forms." Later he said, "'It' is very real and has caused more archers to drop quietly out of archery than any other single reason." Well, "It" has a name—*target panic*. We prefer a slightly less loaded name, namely the British version—*target shyness*, with *shy* here carrying the same meaning it does in the term *gun shy*. *Target panic* seems to be the name that stuck, however.

Today there are archery coaches who have made their careers on treating target panic, whereas others deny it even exists. Some even say, "If you talk about it enough, you'll get it." Target panic is a whole pile of maladies that generally results in poor shooting. Typically, beginners are immune, but virtually all archers who shoot respectable scores get some form of it. It shows up as the involuntarily loosing of shots, or an inability to hold your sight on the target, or freezing while holding on some part of the target other than the part you want to hit. There are other forms as well. Bow hunters generally refer to "It" as "buck fever."

In our opinion, beginners don't get target panic because they tend to improve significantly over time as their form develops and they gain experience. Then they reach a plateau where their scores don't improve so quickly or at all and, instead of trusting their training and practice, they try to "help" improve their scores. When athletes report on what was happening when they were performing at the top of their games, they often say that everything seemed effortless and that the last thing they were thinking about was the execution of their shot. They were just trusting their training and executing. To shoot at all successfully, archers must do the same. Trying to execute an archery shot while at the same time thinking of ways to improve the shot as it is happening is a recipe for disaster.

The good news is that "It" can be cured. In fact, hundreds of archers have done so. If you have "It" now, you can survive it and get back to competitive shooting. We have read about and been taught literally dozens of techniques to solve this problem. If you shoot with your fingers, using a clicker often solves the problem, although there is a form of the malady called clicker panic. If you have a significant problem, you will probably need to "take a cure." These are in the form of a self-treatment program, an example of which is shown in figure 10.1 (courtesy of George Chapman).

FIGURE 10.1 TARGET PANIC TREATMENT ROUTINE

1. Stop shooting in competition.

2. Shoot a large number of arrows a day (e.g., 150 to 200) with your eyes closed (up close to a target butt) for two weeks.

3. Shoot a large number of arrows a day (e.g., 150 to 200) with your eyes open but no bow sight (up close to a target butt) for two weeks.

4. Shoot a large number of arrows a day (e.g., 150 to 200) with your eyes open with a bow sight using a large-diameter ring aperture into a 48-inch target five yards away for two weeks.

5. Move back five yards every two weeks of shooting or switch to smaller targets (depending on how much space you have to shoot in) until you are shooting standard-sized targets from standard distances.

If there are dozens of cures, which should you choose? It depends on your personality. Our best advice is get together with a good coach or successful shooter who has experience working with target panic and try one of the schemes. You will need to find the one that will work for you. Everyone reports different successes with the various techniques. The things these treatments have in common, though, are very telling. They all say that you must not shoot competitively until you've treated yourself successfully. They all take away the target initially and work on the "feel" of a shot or just the execution of a shot without aiming. They all deemphasize scoring when targets are reintroduced. All of these are designed to get you to stop thinking about ways to improve your shot and thereby your score while you are shooting.

Going to the Archery Doctor

We are continually amazed at the attitudes of many archers toward coaches. If you wanted to learn golf or tennis or any other new sport, you would probably sign up for some lessons and expect to pay for them. Then why do so many archers think coaching is superfluous or that $3 an hour is plenty to pay for it? Sorry for the rant, but this is not exactly a new problem. Writing in 1577, Roger Ascham said, "But faults in archers do exceed the number of archers, which are caused by the use of shooting without teaching" (Ascham 1577). Milan Elott wrote in 1963, "In spite of the fact that coaches have been training champions for over thirty years, the average archer of today does not even know such training exists. . . . It never occurs to them that they *can be taught* to shoot" (Elott ca. 1963).

Both the National Archery Association (NAA) and the National Field Archery Association (NFAA) have fine coaching development programs. Contact either one to find a coach in your area.

11

The Joys of Arco Nudo

Ty Pelfrey

Barebow, or *arco nudo* as the Europeans call it, is just as it sounds, a bow without attached sights or lengthy stabilizers. It can be a compound bow or a recurve bow, but since most serious barebow archers shoot an Olympic style recurve bow with a small counterbalance on the lower riser, I will concentrate on this.

Barebow practitioners use modern archery equipment to challenge themselves in ever changing and physically demanding range layouts. Barebow can be shot in "normal" target rounds (i.e., on a flat surface), but reaches its ultimate form in the field where you will find shots uphill and downhill at near impossible angles, and shots where you stand on steep slopes or slippery mud, and even shots into spots you need a rope to climb up to retrieve your arrows. FITA field rounds are not for wimps! Cliffs and extreme downhill shots can be unnerving (see figure 11.1).

Without sights and wheels you have as near naked a bow as they come (see figure 11.2). Armed with your arrow rest, riser, limbs, and counterbalance, you are about ready to begin. Before competing officially, however, read all the rules regarding arrow rests, counterweights, and balances; there are

© Ty Pelfrey

Figure 11.1 Uphill targets, downhill targets, strange footing—all are parts of field archery, the ultimate barebow challenge.

© Ty Pelfrey

Figure 11.2 You get a bow, a string, and maybe a counterbalance—no sight, no stabilizer, no peep sight, and no clicker. The entire bow, unstrung, must pass through a ring 4.8 inches (12.2 centimeters) in diameter.

limits. These can be found on the FITA Web site at www.archery.org/rule_book/rule_book.html.

Getting Started

A few archers still shoot the one-piece wood recurve in the barebow division, but most archers have chosen the take-down recurve. Bow poundage is not limited. An informal survey of the men's bows at the 2000 World Field Championships in Cortina, Italy, noted bows ranging from 35 to 45 pounds of draw. The female barebow archers had comparable bows. My personal setup includes a set of 40-pound limbs, a 5-pound reduction from last year's setup. With a little experimentation and a lot of practice, I noticed that a lighter arrow compensated for the loss of poundage, and my form improved. Hopefully my scores will follow suit!

The length of the limbs and bow poundage are critical for a good bow tune. The longer the bow, the less string pinch you have because of a larger string angle at full draw. You'll want a comfortable bow when you shoot on those steep mountain passes. Most barebow archers shoot 66- to 70-inch long bows. Since barebow archers "walk the string," having longer limbs is considered desirable by some. For example, a 68-inch bow can be made with a 23-inch riser and long limbs or a 25-inch riser and medium length limbs. The first combination would be the more desirable. Some barebow archers, however, will argue the merits the other way.

Arrows. All arrows must be the same length and have the same color fletch or design. There is a limit on the maximum diameter of the shaft, but you'll probably want a small-diameter shaft that is fast and consistent and provides minimal surface area to combat shifting alpine winds. Tough Carbon Tech® shafts with Kurly Vanes/Spin Wing type vanes and tunable nocks are great for field archery. Easton A/C/E, A/C/C, and X10 shaft systems are also popular with barebow shooters. Don't forget to write your name on the shafts—it is the rule.

Quiver. The competitive barebow archer requires a quality quiver to carry a dozen arrows, tools, and a bow hook. Field course shooters will be walking up and down hills, so a deep side quiver with separate arrow tubes helps keep the arrows separated and eases unnecessary wear on the arrow fletches. Tool pockets and a place for your arrow puller is a good idea. Water bottle holders are also handy.

Optics. Binoculars or a monocular are great tools to see targets in shaded positions or to spot your arrows. Optics that allow you to range targets are not allowed on official field rounds, but any standard pair of optics can be carried during a tournament. We'll talk about ranging and why these optics are important later. Grab your current set of binoculars; they'll do just fine.

Clothing and Gear. Field tournaments may be postponed or canceled because of lightning, but rain or snow only make the course more challenging. Because of the variations in weather, the dress code allows blue denim and rain gear but absolutely no camouflage clothing (safety in the woods). Dress for extreme conditions and warm, sunny days in the field. Always consider safety when going out to the range.

Once you leave the staging area and begin a FITA field round, you may be on the course until your 24 target round is completed. You could be out four to six hours. Seasoned shooters carry a small backpack with a built-in foldout chair, snacks, and water.

The Road Less Traveled

FITA field courses are typically on steep, uneven, wooded terrain. Walking and standing, not to mention shooting, can be difficult. There is no limit on shot angles at a tournament, as long as they are considered safe. Two archers share a blue shooting stake throughout each day's competition. You'll have a comfortable four minutes to catch your breath and shoot each three-arrow end. In this case, here's what to expect on a FITA field course. I will also discuss how to prepare for the various uphill and downhill targets and the scoring rings on a FITA field face.

Ribbons tied to branches or trees thread through the forest or desert linking targets to establish a FITA field course. This is similar to an NFAA field course, minus the trails, comfortable walking, benches, bow racks, and mild shot angles. Don't plan on using straw bales as a part of your aiming system; most field rounds use circular mats of different sizes to confuse archers on the unmarked round.

Arrow attrition and archer entertainment seem to be a side goal of most course organizers. You may find yourself shooting at an uphill target placed on a rock cliff face at a mild 45-degree angle. That shot could be followed by a target mat placed in the fork of a pine tree with nothing but blue sky as a backdrop; a missed arrow will be swallowed by an uninhabited section of forest. The footing can be muddy and slick. Rest assured; many target butts will be nestled in unforgiving basalt, granite, or other indigenous stone. Remember that you get three attempts per target, so carry plenty of arrows.

The field round lends itself to a two-day tournament. The first day is spent shooting at 24 targets. Actual distances to the targets are not stated. Field archers must determine the size of the face and then estimate the distance to the target. (FITA rule books state the established target distance parameters.) There are red-staked shooting positions and blue-staked shooting positions on the range. Barebow archers are to shoot close to, and behind, the blue stakes. Our compound friends and Olympic recurve partners shoot from the red stakes. (See tables 11.1 and 11.2 for distance charts.)

Day two consists of the 24 target marked round, on a separate course. On day two the distances from the blue stakes to the target are provided in meters.

TABLE 11.1   4.5.3.7 UNIT FOR UNMARKED COURSE

Number of targets	Diameter of field faces (cm)	Blue peg barebow (m)	Red peg recurve and compound (m)
3	20	5-10	10-15
3	40	10-20	15-25
3	60	15-30	20-35
3	80	30-45	35-55

TABLE 11.2   4.5.3.8 UNIT FOR MARKED COURSE

Number of targets	Diameter of field faces (cm)	Blue peg barebow (m)	Red peg recurve and compound (m)
3	20	5-10-15	10-15-20
3	40	15-20-25	20-25-30
3	60	30-35-40	35-40-45
3	80	40-45-50	50-55-60

Remember to stand behind the stake and not beyond your blue gauntlet during the three-arrow end. The red stakes are reserved for Olympic recurve and compound shooters. In all there are 48 targets shot over two days of competition. National and international competitions offer additional targets for elimination, final, and medal rounds.

Scoring on Target

FITA field targets consist of a black face with white lines separating the scoring regions. A gold center indicates the five ring with its inner X ring (see figure 11.3). You only need to break or touch a line with the arrow shaft to score the higher point value. You are allowed three shots and four minutes at the blue stake. Take your time and use your optics to check your range and windage. As in any round, miss and you might break an arrow. As for the score of a *missed* arrow, record it as an *M* on the scorecard.

There are four sizes of targets with maximum and minimum distances associated with each target size (see tables 11.1 and 11.2). The 20-centimeter and 40-centimeter target faces are easily

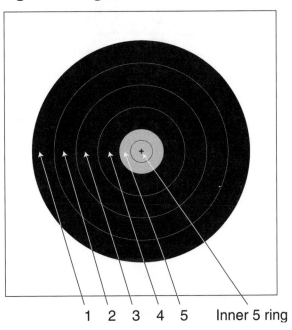

1   2   3   4   5   Inner 5 ring

Figure 11.3 A FITA field target face and its score values. The 5-ring is gold/yellow and the rest is black
Reprinted, by permission, from FITA, *FITA Constitution and Rules* (Online). Available http://www.archery.org/ (June 8, 2003).

distinguished because of their layouts on the target butt (see figure 11.4). The 60-centimeter and 80-centimeter faces are the ones that cause ranging difficulty, especially when situated in dark forested hollows or on gleaming mountain peaks. Even rookies can sound like experts if they refer to the 20-centimeter faces as "bunnies" or "birdies."

Shooting Uphill and Downhill

Practicing uphill and downhill shots is important for barebow shooters and any archer interested in challenging terrain. See figure 4.7 on page 60 for a chart to assist archers. You will typically need to add or deduct yardage for uphill and downhill shots. Remember that no charts are allowed on the range, so practice, practice, practice!

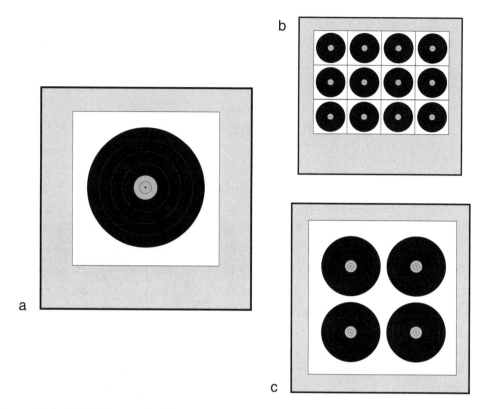

Figure 11.4 Typical layouts for FITA field faces, including *(a)* 80 and 60 cm faces; *(b)* 20 cm faces; and *(c)* 40 cm faces

Reprinted, by permission, from FITA, *FITA Constitution and Rules* (Online). Available http://www.archery.org/ (June 8, 2003).

You can make an inexpensive angle finder from a carpenter's angle finder and a piece of arrow shaft or buy a more expensive clinometer to visualize various shot angles. Now you can use the angle chart and experiment with your equipment. Results will vary with the addition or deduction of yardage for various uphill and downhill challenges. Practice!

Peak physical condition is a must. Shooting various uphill and downhill combinations will challenge the muscles in your back, arms, and legs. Develop a stretching program and exercise regime to strengthen those little-used muscles (see chapter 5).

An acquaintance of mine hangs a target from his garage rafters for uphill shooting practice. The same archer also stands on his roof to practice shooting straight down at the *birdie* targets placed on a target butt in his driveway. These are extreme practice techniques, but he is a licensed contractor and can fix his roof when he misses. Consider safety in all practice situations.

Estimating Distance

Practice, practice, and more practice. That's the answer. The question is, How do you judge the distance to the target? The barebow enthusiast needs a small bag of tricks to accurately estimate the distance to the unmarked targets and an aiming system to put points on the scorecard.

Unmarked targets are set out within maximum and minimum ranges, but you must determine the *actual* distance to the target. Estimating the distance to targets is as much science as it is art. Shadows from tall timber, shots across mountain ravines, undulating terrain, and target faces mounted off perpendicular all offer a twist to the distance estimation chore.

Some shooters gaze at a path to the target and flip meter sticks over and over in their minds. Other shooters imagine a grid of five-meter squares and estimate. One shooter I know imagines himself walking to the target; he counts his imaginary steps. These are only some of the estimation tricks. Knowing that the target faces are standard sizes is helpful. Being able to see the white scoring rings is even more helpful (binoculars do help). Electronic or mechanical range finders are not allowed in a tournament, but for practice they are invaluable for checking your distance estimation skills.

When I decided to take my FITA field scores more seriously, I studied my mentor, Mark Applegate. Mark is one of the best barebow archers in the United States and holds a dozen U.S. national championships. His solid archery form, mental toughness, and practice schedule are a few of the reasons his arrows often find the target's center. Mark patiently listened to my ranging theories, but was quiet on the issue. His exasperating patience gave me the opportunity to *earn* the value of a technique that was passed on to him. Conservatively, the range estimation learning curve cost me two dozen carbon arrows and gave my mentor quite a few chuckles. Finally, in a whispered tone, he gave me the ranging gift I was looking for. Thanks, Mark.

To learn the skill, you need to practice looking at, and shooting, the different sized faces. Estimating distance to within a meter is essential for competitive success and personal growth in FITA field rounds. Purchase the latest FITA rule book for rules on shot sequence and target rotation, and detailed rules on equipment and scoring.

Aiming—The Golden Point

Barebow shooters use a combination of techniques to aim. Some shooters change face anchors and walk the string; others walk the string and use the point of their arrow as an aiming tool. Still others walk the string and use various pieces of their bows as aiming devices. Most competitive shooters walk the string.

String walking is changing the location of your fingers on the string. Moving your fingers down the string raises the back end of the arrow and lowers the trajectory of the arrow. The archer typically sights across the tip of the arrow.

When you discuss string walking, other practitioners, or your coach, may ask, "What is your *point on target distance?*" The question is, How far back from the target must you stand so that, on level ground, and sighting across your arrow point at the center of the target, the arrow hits that center? You'll need to know your "point on."

String walkers place their fingers close to the nock for long shots and move their fingers farther down the string for closer in shots. The right place on the string to pull the bow is called "the crawl." Hang on; give me a few more paragraphs and a few illustrations to describe the concept. You are going to like what you see!

Go get your bow and use it as a visualization tool for the next few paragraphs. Here's how walking the string works. Place three fingers on the string below a nocked arrow (see figure 11.5a). Pull the string back to your anchor. Try anchoring at the corner of your mouth or cheek instead of using an Olympic-style (under the chin) anchor. Sight past the tip of the arrow at the desired target. At my "point on target" distance I see the top of my index finger against the bottom of the nock; at full draw the tip of my arrow is on the gold and I see my bowstring hovering on the outside edge of my bow riser. The aforementioned setup will cast my Carbon Tech 210 arrows from my 40-pound limb, 68-inch Sky Conquest bow exactly 50 meters on level ground (given that I aim and execute the shot as I have been taught). This is my "point on."

Now slide your fingers below the nock two inches (see figure 11.5b). Pull the bow back to the same anchor point you used when you had the top of your index finger against the nock (see figure 11.5c). Congratulations, you just walked the string! This is a typical sight picture, walking the string, for a five-meter target. Put the tip of the arrow on the gold. The arrow point is your sight. For close targets, the string alignment may need to be more centered on the riser, or it may remain the same.

Walking the string is simply changing your finger position on the string, which changes the angle of the arrow in reference to your aiming eye. The goal for serious string walkers is to be able to shoot all of the distances (5 to 50 meters) while having their fingers as close to the nock as possible. The longer the crawl on the string, the more difficulty there is in tuning the bow for good arrow flight (see the discussion of arrow tuning in chapter 7). In the current example, you will need to crawl the string between the nock and your five-meter mark to find the other distances. These are your sight marks.

Some string walkers count the monofilament serving strands below their nocking point with their thumbnail to determine the exact placement of the finger tab on the string. Braided serving is a little tougher wearing, but doesn't offer the audible click of a thumbnail flowing over each individual strand of

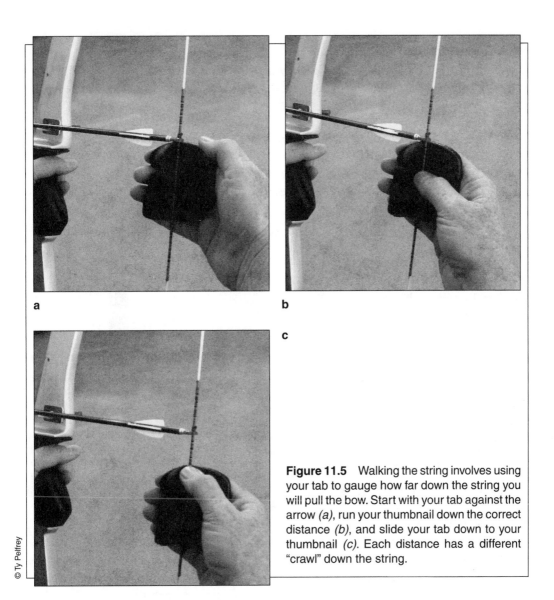

a

b

c

© Ty Pelfrey

Figure 11.5 Walking the string involves using your tab to gauge how far down the string you will pull the bow. Start with your tab against the arrow *(a)*, run your thumbnail down the correct distance *(b)*, and slide your tab down to your thumbnail *(c)*. Each distance has a different "crawl" down the string.

serving. Shooters who use braided servings usually have another technique to measure their crawls, such as using tab stitches, finger grooves, or the recessed metal screw heads that hold their tab together, to measure the distance down the string.

Other archers memorize the layout of the stitches on their finger tab and the various target distances associated with each stitch. Five meters might be an inch and a half (seven stitches) below the nock to the top of the finger tab. Aiming at a target 40 meters away may only require the archer to slide the tab down the string a quarter inch (one stitch).

Shooting Off the Shelf

Some string walkers use two sighting references. A common practice is called "shooting off the shelf." This technique is best illustrated with a picture (see figure 11.6). Archers who use the shelf as an aiming point find that there is about a 20-meter difference from this aiming point and the tip of their arrow. If you can use your fingers against the nock and shoot 50 meters using the tip of your arrow, you will be able to shoot about 70 meters using the shelf to aim with.

The advantage to shooting off the shelf is that you can tune your bow so the point on is at 25 meters, a good midrange place. Then string walkers retain that good bow tune and elevate their aiming picture to the shelf and shoot 45 to 50 meters. Tuning the bow-arrow system with no crawl is much easier than trying to find a tune that works for a wide range of crawls. Using the shelf minimizes the radical changes in arrow dynamics as you creep down the string. Just don't forget to use the shelf, and not the arrow point, on the longer targets, or your arrows will stick in the dirt 25 meters distant and well short of the target. That's one of those free tips that cost me a few carbon arrows to learn!

Figure 11.6 Wherever the fuzzy image of the string appears on the bow riser, you must have it in the same place each time for consistency. Moving the string's alignment affects the left-right impact point of your arrows.

Multiple Anchors

Still other barebow shooters change where they anchor on their face to compensate for the different distances. String walkers can grip the string with three fingers and hold with the index finger in the corner of their mouth. To change the trajectory of the arrow, and thus the sight mark, they can anchor with their middle finger at the corner of their mouth. Typically, archers find a 20-meter decrease in point on when they change from an index to a middle finger anchor. This technique has similar benefits when shooting off the shelf.

Athletic string-walkers use two fingers instead of three to hold the bowstring at full draw. This technique offers a smoother release, but increased finger fatigue.

Horizontal Tune

Once you begin to experiment with moving your fingers up and down the string, you may notice different arrow impact patterns. On some distances your arrows pattern left or right of the spot. You'll need to experiment with string alignment. You may need to align the image of your string on the *inside* of your riser for close shots and the *outside* for long shots, and *on* the riser for middle distance shots (see figure 11.6). String alignment will vary with bow length, archer draw, arrow length, arrow spine, anchor, and about two dozen other variables. Play with the string alignment. Having a rear horizontal reference is great!

Archers are always looking for the perfect tab or leather for the perfect tab. Medical casting tape and other synthetics are also being used to protect the fingers of barebow archers in conjunction with tabs, or without a shooting tab. Seldom have I seen a serious barebow archer who uses a glove to protect the fingers.

Continued experimentation with anchors and finger placement on the string will reveal the best combination. Then you memorize them!

An adjustable cushion plunger to work with your arrow rest is essential for fine-tuning and accurate barebow shooting. Beiter and other companies make great products for this application.

Tuning the bow to accommodate such radical anchors and aiming techniques is a time-intensive, limb bolt–turning, string-twisting, and plunger-adjusting process. Take good written notes; just don't take them into competition.

The entire unbraced barebow, including any weights, must slide through the judge's official ring that is 12.2 centimeters (4.8 inches) in diameter. The shooting official will also have you draw your bow during inspection to make sure the bowstring's center serving doesn't end within the aiming eye's vision (no informal rear sights are allowed!).

Shots on the level, like those of an Olympic round, are few and far between. Seldom will field archers find comfortable level footing. I highly recommend a pair of instep ice crampons for traction on slippery surfaces. The extra spikes strapped to your boots will help you stay on the mountain during the shot sequence.

Practice Ranges and Targets

Calculating shot angles and shooting on sidehill grades are two additional art forms that must be mastered before venturing into friendly competition. Yea, more practice! Find a friend with a mountain, or try public lands. Consider the safety of your shooting at all times. Using portable foam targets and lightweight metal stands is an efficient way to set up ever changing field courses and practice ranges.

My favorite practice range is a huge granite boulder jumble at six thousand feet in California's Sierra Nevada. Huge rocks and sheer cliffs allow severe uphill and downhill angles. Shifting winds and thin air simulate FITA field tournament conditions. The hillside also allows me to shoot downhill with my toes pointing uphill and uphill with my toes pointing downhill. The multitude of body angles and shooting positions makes field rounds very challenging and fresh.

The Naked Barebow Truth

The camaraderie among the participants in the barebow division is heart warming. Information on techniques and equipment is readily shared (sometimes earned) in the spirit of propelling the sport, and its participants, to new heights.

Imagine yourself perched on a lush mountainside with your bow at full draw. The wind buffets your body, and your arrow point meanders around the target's yellow center. Rain threatens on the horizon. The string slips from your fingers, and the arrow sails toward the target. The shot was perfect! You look over your shoulder, and your shooting partners smile.

For those willing to take the time to tune their equipment, practice, and ask questions (lots of them), barebow can be a rewarding experience.

12

Perfecting Practice

When Steve first got into archery, his idea of practice was to shoot some arrows. If he shot a lot of arrows, that was a lot of practice. If he shot only a few, that was a little practice. He thought he could practice a little and then go compete. How hard could it be? When winter came, his bow got packed away not to be touched until spring. Each spring was like starting over because his muscles and mind were both lax. Now Steve has practice sessions in the fall in which he sets up equipment he will shoot indoors over the winter. These sessions are interspersed with practice sessions focused on the current season's equipment tuning, form tuning, and body tuning (weight and cardio training). And he moans about not having enough time to practice. He never practices by just shooting arrows at targets. How do you practice? Do you have a plan?

Practicing to Fail

An old saying is, Failing to practice is practicing to fail. But we have discovered that you can practice to fail without failing to practice. If your practice sessions are not focused, if you don't have an objective for your practice, if your practice is not directed at what you will be doing and under what conditions, you may be practicing to fail.

Steve Ruis and Claudia Stevenson

When Steve attended his first FITA competition, he looked up all of the rules and consulted people on what to expect. He got some FITA targets and measured off the distances to make sure everything worked with those targets. But until he got some practice shooting against a clock (the NFAA rules we normally shot under didn't time shots), he didn't understand what was involved. He needed to know how many times he could let down and still get off three good shots in two minutes or six good shots in four minutes. He didn't realize that he could get off a reasonable shot even though it didn't feel right if the alternative was not getting a shot off at all and scoring zero. He also felt what it was like not to get the shot off in time. That was a valuable practice session!

Try an experiment. At your next practice session log everything you do and how many minutes you take to do it. When we did this, we found that sometimes almost half of our practices were, at best, social time. Yes, we were talking with fellow archers, sometimes about subjects unrelated to archery. So, even if you are practicing, that practice may not be pointing you to success (however you define it).

Elements of Successful Practice

If you have a goal (winning a particular tournament, shooting a personal best score, shooting a FITA round with all arrows scoring), your practice sessions should help you achieve it. You may believe, for example, that shooting arrows prepares you physically to pull your bow. But shooting arrows at a target may not be the only way to develop the muscles you need to draw your bow. Weight training or reversal training may be better. (Reversal training is merely drawing a heavier draw bow than the one you shoot and holding at full draw for a number of seconds and doing this a number of times per session. We have no idea why this is called *reversal* training.)

Archers often break down their shots into discussible, addressable pieces. Yes, the shot is really one continuous action, but talking about a one-piece shot is difficult. What we are talking about here is your form and your shot sequence. Some of the pro shooters we know say they are working on relaxation. What they really mean is that they are working on relaxing their drawing arm biceps muscles at full draw. Some spend several hours drawing in front of a blank bale, not shooting, just focusing on relaxing their biceps. One thing at a time indeed!

Practice sessions, then, break down into three types—form practice, equipment setup and tuning, and tournament preparation. If you aren't working on your form, or working on your equipment, or preparing for a tournament, you are probably wasting your time or, worse, practicing to get *worse*!

- **Form practice.** When you are practicing your form or execution, practice one thing at a time. When you are working on any particular aspect of your shot sequence, that is form practice. When you trying to relax a set of muscles while shooting, that is form practice. The majority of your practice time is generally going to be form practice.

- **Equipment setup and tuning.** When setting up and tuning your equipment, you again need to work on only one thing at a time. If you change three settings on your bow simultaneously, you won't know which of them was responsible for any improvement. One adjustment may have worked really well, but another may have offset some of that great improvement so that you got only a small improvement. Make one change at a time and see how each works. Be sure to read chapter 13, "Testing New Equipment."

- **Tournament preparation.** Everything you do is preparing you to compete one way or another, but here we are talking about preparing for a specific tournament. This may include shooting practice rounds that are identical or similar to those of the tournament. It may include trying to simulate the atmosphere of the shoot site. If you expect many distractions, for example, you may want to get a friend to talk to you or otherwise try to distract you while you are shooting. If the tournament involves a field course with many uphill and downhill shots, you may want to find some hills to practice on. If the tournament site is windy . . . you get the idea.

Planning to Practice

Developing a practice plan isn't easy. Coaches can help, but there are some limitations. You can't tune better than you shoot, for example. So, the goal is to bring up all aspects of your shooting together. Consequently, you don't want to leave out, say, tuning, because shooting an untuned bow will give you a false impression of the effectiveness of your form. You don't want to leave mental skills practice out, thinking you can do that later, because mental skills failings can look like form or execution failings, and then you will end up practicing the wrong things. Your practice plan needs to include *all* of the elements of successful shooting—physical training, mental training, equipment preparation, and competition.

Physical Training

Do you fatigue during shoots? Does your bow arm drop? Do you collapse at full draw? Again, a coach's or shooting partner's input can be invaluable in helping you to plan your physical training regime. Along with strength training, you must address cardiovascular fitness. Many competitions last all day or many days. Do you finish as strong as you started? See chapter 5 for a good idea of what is involved. Schedule whatever exercises you will be doing and then stick to the plan!

Mental Training

Chapter 6 will help you develop a mental skills plan. Again, you must stick to the plan. This is not something you do as last minute practice; you need to practice mental skills until they are habit. This may be as simple as the technique of faking a big yawn when you get irritated or too aroused to shoot well. It works (try it!), but if you don't do it as a matter of habit, you won't be likely to think to do it when it is needed. Make mental skills part of your practice regimen.

Equipment Preparation

If you are a sponsored shooter, your sponsors may send you a bow when you don't expect one and expect you to use it. They want feedback from you about what works and doesn't work, and they want you to be seen with their cool, new bow. Should you change? If you aren't in the midst of tournament preparation and you don't have to cannibalize your old setup, you could schedule some tuning sessions with the new gear. As long as it doesn't interfere in a major way with your practice plan, it may put a better piece of equipment in your toolkit.

If you are buying your own bow, when is the best time to do so—right before the most important tournament of the season, or between seasons so you have time to evaluate it? We all have a story or two about some archer who got a new bow two days before a big tournament, threw it together, and won. Some people win the lottery, too. The question is, are you one of those people?

Equipment preparation, one of the three modes of practice, requires time and a lot of note taking.

Competition

The best environment to practice in so that you will be good in competition is—you got it—competitions. Minor competitions can be used as tune-ups for major ones. We have both shot major tournaments for the experience of being at that tournament. That is, we went without expectations and with the plan of focusing on the total experience so that when we came back we would be familiar with the format and the looks, feels, and smells of the venue. Sometimes archers go to a competition to work on just one aspect of shooting in a competitive environment. Archers with that intention have even focused so well on practicing that they shot a personal best or even won!

One of the charms of target archery is that so many of the national championships are open tournaments, which means that you don't have to qualify. If you can get there and have the tournament fees, you are in! (This is how Claudia and I attended our first national championship shoot in 1997. She came in second in her class; I came in eleventh. Hers was from the top, mine was from the bottom, but my goal was to not come in last. Hers was to win!) So you can compete at the national level! The question is, though, can you be competitive?

Newcomers can, and do, win on their first try. It helps if there is no one else in their category! This often happens to kids at their first shoot. It may have happened to you. It is not at all common for adults, though.

One of the reasons most people like to travel is to experience new and interesting things. Each of those new things, however, takes some time to assimilate. Too many new things all at once can be disorienting and no fun. The first time you attend a tournament, *everything* is new and different. Consequently, it is hard to turn off your brain's self-defense mechanisms to focus completely on shooting. (Your brain always evaluates anything new for its potential to threaten your safety.)

The archers who come to a tournament with a chance of winning are usually those who already have a lot of tournament experience; only part of what is going on is new to them. The biggest obstacle to success for beginners is tournament pressure.

Occasionally someone makes a big splash by doing really well at his or her first national-level tournament, but this doesn't usually happen. Typically, tournament pressure (Dang, I am competing to be U.S. Champion!) causes beginners to crumple like aluminum foil.

Practice Is Fun!

Let's face it: If practice weren't fun, you wouldn't do it. Basically, it is your job to make it fun, and to do so you will need to know a little about yourself. If you are a social animal, you are going to want to have a practice partner (or partners). These are not just people to shoot with but friends who will help keep you centered on meeting your practice goals. They can try to distract you while you are shooting so you can learn to deal with distractions. They can also compete with you. Try giving them a number of points as a handicap in a round that will make it difficult, but possible, to beat them, and then place a bet such as the loser washes the other's car.

If you are a loner, make up novel ways to interest and challenge yourself. Use a photocopy machine to make smaller-than-normal targets to shoot at. Try shooting in a completely different venue to pique your interest. Start identifying the things you find fun so you can incorporate them into your practice plans.

13

Testing New Equipment

New gear is one of the sources of joy for archers. Christmas can be in July if that is when your new bow is delivered. When faced with new equipment, you may wonder how to proceed. Do you strip your old bow to set up the new one? Taking the adage of "fools rush in where angels fear to tread" to heart, it seems good advice to proceed slowly. Have you ever cut a set of brand new arrows too short? If you have, you are not alone; online auctions often have dozens of arrows for sale labeled "Oops, cut too short—my mistake may be your windfall" or some other such comment. This chapter will guide you in checking out new equipment.

A Fool and His Money

We are going to push two things that you should think about and push them hard. One is "try before you buy." The other is "compare the new with the old." Advertisers use psychology to convince us that *new* and *improved* equals *better*. It ain't necessarily so. It is also often true. You can buy better scores!

We have heard coach after coach hammering on one thing: You can't buy better scores! But you *know* you can. Take the simple case of replacing a set of mismatched, bent arrows

Steve Ruis and Claudia Stevenson

with a brand new set correctly spined for your bow. The new arrows will be more consistent, which means you will shoot more consistently and improve your score. What these coaches are trying to tell you, however, is that once your equipment is set up adequately for you, only marginal improvements can be had through better equipment. Most archers will be far better off working on form and execution as sources of better scores.

Some Basics

Being set up adequately means that you have an appropriately sized bow that has a manageable draw weight that allows you to reach all of the distances you shoot. It means that you have dependable accessories (sights, clickers, releases, tabs, etc.) and appropriate arrows spined for your bow and your form. If you are a compound archer, you will also need a bow with the correct draw length. If you have all of these, a new gizmo will have only a marginal impact on your ability to perform.

Realize, though, that when you are looking for every little advantage in competition, a 1-percent increase in score may be significant. If you are an intermediate or "just made advanced" archer, however, you might be better off spending your money on coaching.

If you are a 6-foot, 4-inch recurve archer shooting a 64-inch bow, getting a 70-inch or even a 72-inch bow could be a real boost. If your arrows fit you and your setup but are relatively heavy, a set of carbon fiber arrows would probably improve your score. If the release you are shooting is very, very fast and you worry about it going off too soon all the time, getting a release that can be adjusted to your shooting style will definitely improve your scores.

For a purchase to have a significant impact on your scores or performance, it must address a significant weakness in your setup—bow fit, arrow spine, arrow weight, something relatively important. Can changing from one manufacturer's carbon arrow to another's of the same mass and spine have much of an effect? For elite archers, maybe. For shooters like you and the two of us, don't count on it.

A coach can be very cost effective in helping you determine whether your equipment or your technique is holding your scores down. You can spend a lot of money trying to correct a form flaw that has nothing to do with your equipment. A coach can see what you can't feel, so find a coach to help.

Try Before You Buy

With all of the bows, arrows, arrow rests, release aids, and so forth on the market, you obviously can't expect to buy one of each to compare. We recommend that you start with what you can afford, and everyone we know can afford to borrow from a friend. Since your friend does not have your exact body size, shape, and shooting style, however, at some point you will want your own gear. You can buy new or used. Either way, you will need some technical help to get your equipment fitted to you and working properly. If you do not have some excellent technical help available in a local archery shop, don't even think about buying used.

You should expect to pay around $40 per hour to have an experienced bow mechanic work on your bow. A $100 bow that needs six hours of work may not be a bargain. A $100 bow that needs six hours of work when there is no bow mechanic nearby is a disaster. If you try to distort your form to use an ill-fitted bow, you will probably drop into the "no fun zone" and quit archery because you won't be able to hit the broad side of a barn.

Get professional help if you can. We hope you have a good archery shop nearby and that they have experienced staff to help you make correct choices of equipment. You may also want to ask people if you can

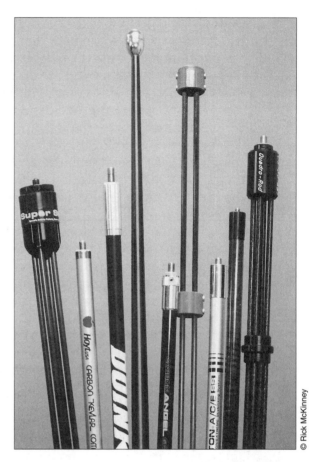

There are literally hundreds of different stabilizers. Which should you use? Try as many as you can by borrowing them from fellow archers before you spend up to $100-$200 on your own.

try their gear. Many of the archers we know regularly lend out arrows, bows, releases, quivers, and other equipment to fellow shooters. Not all archers will agree to such a request, however. Every archer we know has some horror story of how some novice dry fired their bow or shot one of their expensive arrows into a concrete wall. If people say "I'd rather not" to your request, just say thank you and move on. It doesn't mean anything. Never draw or even touch someone's bow without permission. This is a definite no-no. Also, if you damage or destroy something you've borrowed, you are obligated to replace it.

If people do respond favorably to your request, we think you are now obligated to pass it on, as it were. When people ask you if they can borrow or try something, try to find a way to say yes.

You can also go to a pro shop to try out equipment. Most shops have a shooting range or a test bale or two for you to try out gear. Don't just grab stuff and start shooting; ask permission first. Also, how much testing you will be able to do is related to how good a customer you are or have been. Nothing irritates a shop owner more than someone who comes into his shop and spends hours testing out stuff (with hours of help thrown in) and then buys on the Internet to save 10 bucks! Have some respect for the shop owner's time and investment. All that help you got is worth something. If the shop's price is reasonably near the price you were hoping to pay, spend your dollars in the place that gives you the best service. If you don't, don't be surprised when you come back to find a grumpy owner who doesn't want to help you because you don't want to help him or, worse, an empty storefront.

Perhaps you normally shoot aluminum arrows and you want to try carbon arrows. Again, trying before you buy is smart, but there are a lot of variables in getting a good arrow-bow tune. Evaluating borrowed arrows can be difficult because you probably aren't going to be able to modify them much. The variables are arrow material (set when you select a type, brand, and model), the arrow's length and spine, the point mass, the fletching mass, the fletching type, the fletching pattern, and the nock type. When you try something that is quite a departure from your normal setup, look around to see what other archers are using. You won't see many field archers who shoot into straw bales with Kurly Vanes or Spin Wings® because "pass-throughs" will rip the vanes off. Similarly, you won't see FITA freestyle archers using five-inch feathers on their arrows (too much drag). What you are looking for is the collective wisdom of all of the shooters of that style. The key here is to try for a "normal" setup. Reasonable point weights, vanes, nocks, and so on should be based on what most people use. The big change here is in the arrow material, so try to keep all other variables "middle of the road." Then select an arrow shaft whose spine is comparable to the spine of the arrows you have been using successfully. With all of the variables near what you have been using, the big difference will be the arrow material, which will translate into reduced arrow mass. Generally, carbon arrows weigh less than equivalently spined aluminum arrows, and you should get more cast or arrow speed.

Be careful not to cut those shafts to the same length you have been using; give yourself a margin for error. Cut them one to two inches longer than your old arrows and shoot test them. If they test weak (likely), then you can cut half an inch off and test them again. If you cut them too short, there is little you can do to weaken them enough to make up for that lack of length. (If you are a compound archer, adding one to three pounds of draw weight might do the trick. Adjusting draw weight can correct for minor errors of judgment.) Once you find the combination that works for you, stick with it.

Compare the New With the Old

So, you've borrowed some different arrows and you want to test them out. If you just go shoot them, you will run afoul of the law that says that everything new seems to work better at first. Your delight at looking at new gear is bound to improve your scores, and you will probably shoot better for a few sessions when you first try it out. You may be more focused, or you may be trying harder; there are any number of reasons for this. If you really want to know if the new gear is better than the old, you have to profile the old and compare it with the new.

Let's say you are a FITA freestyle shooter and a buddy has lent you a set of limbs the same draw weight and length as your limbs, but made by a different company and reputed to be "faster." If you throw them on your riser and fling a few sets of arrows, you won't learn much. What you need to do is to profile your old setup. Take a set of log pages that have target faces printed on them with you to the practice range. Shoot what you think are good arrows at all of the distances you normally shoot and mark the targets with the impact points of the arrows. Then switch limbs. Because two pairs of identical limbs from the same manufacturer would be considered a minor miracle, the odds are that these limbs (being from different manufacturers) are different from your old ones. But what is the difference? Is it big enough to warrant the expense of buying a pair?

Because the limbs are different, you may need to retune, but go ahead and shoot some groups anyway. If your groups are smaller (indicating more consistent characteristics) and higher on the targets (indicating more cast and arrow speed), these are probably better limbs. How much better depends on how much cast or consistency you get. Also, you may need to shoot these limbs quite a bit to evaluate their feel. Some limbs reduce the feel of the shot and are not desirable (or are more desirable) on that account. Some produce too much vibration. Some limbs "stack" excessively; that is, the draw force goes up at a faster rate at the end of the draw (exactly where you don't want this). Some limbs improve performance at longer distances rather than shorter, or vice versa. Once you've compared the two, write something in your log about the feel of your original setup versus the feel of the new setup.

If you have to retune to get good groups, the evaluation becomes more difficult. Is any observed performance difference due to the limbs or to a better tune of the equipment? If you think it is just a better tune, put your old limbs back on and try for that better tune. If you can't find that better tune, maybe the new limbs are more "tunable." Only you can decide if they are worth the price at this point. You can see that taking careful notes can be a tremendous aid in sorting out such a problem.

Steve tells the story of getting some new arrows (same brand, same size), fletching them identically to the old set, and inserting the same points; everything was the same. But the new arrows grouped an inch to an inch and a half below the old ones at 40 yards. He tried rotating the nocks. He tried putting new nocks on his old arrows (the old arrows' worn nocks may have been coming off the string more easily). He then shared his conundrum with his mentor, Rusty Mills. "Let me see some of each set," said Rusty. He looked at them and stood them all on their points on a flat surface. The new arrows were half an inch longer than the old ones! Steve had always shot that arrow uncut from the factory, but the factory decided to supply those shafts a half an inch longer than before. Compare the new with the old, indeed! Here are some other examples of how you can make the most of your archery budget.

- **Testing out a new release.** Testing out a release can be difficult unless you are allowed to make adjustments. A difference of a quarter inch in the length of a release rope changes your draw length by that much (or requires you to compensate for the change). What you are looking for is the proper fit. If a wrist strap is involved, does it fit your wrist comfortably? Is it snug enough so that it won't slip? Do the parts that go in your hand fit your hand? Your hand needs to be relaxed, but if the release spreads your fingers way out, you won't be able to relax it. Does the release trigger with very little travel? Can you "punch" it if necessary? Is the trigger pressure adjustable?

  Always test a new release aid up close to a bale without a target until you get used to it. A release that triggers halfway through the draw cycle can result in you punching yourself silly.

- **Trying out a new finger tab.** Tabs are inexpensive, usually have to be shot quite a bit to evaluate them, and need to be trimmed a bit to make them fit just right. For these reasons you should just buy one that you want to try.

- **Trying out a new stabilizer.** By all means, borrow what you can. Stabilizers can cost hundreds of dollars, and a borrowed one can be tested without much modification. Be sure to check with the lender to find out how much change he or she will tolerate (e.g., changing end weights or vee bars or repositioning tunable sliding weights).

In Closing

We hope this chapter has given you some guidance as to how to make the best decisions on archery gear. We both admit that if it hadn't been for generous friends, we would never have gotten into archery. We borrowed *everything* to begin with, then bought tabs, arrows, and sights. Eventually we bought our own bows, binoculars, stabilizers, and so forth. We pass on the gift that was given us by lending and selling inexpensively our older equipment to archers just getting into the sport. We hope you will do the same.

14

Embracing the Spirit of Archery

At the end of a book on *how* comes the question *why*. Why do we bother with archery? We have learned to hit the bull's-eye, so why do we spend our precious time and energy working to hit it more often? Why bother hitting it at all? How could we possibly benefit from this archaic skill?

My good friend Jim often complains that if he had put the same amount of work into something other than archery, he'd be rich! Or fluent in French, or have a PhD in the subject of his choice, or . . . . He'd certainly have *something* to show for all of his effort. But there he is (yes, probably right this very minute) out at the range working on the "one next thing" that will improve his ability to consistently hit that spot. Is he crazy? Maybe. But it's worth a look at what archery offers us that makes us pick up our bows again and again.

Self-Knowledge

Some of us shoot because we love the competition; others want something that provides relaxation and physical activity. Still others shoot simply to spend time with a loved one who happens to be an archery nut. But once you put that bow in your hand, you are learning about you—your "self." What could be more fascinating than that?

Claudia Stevenson

At first it may be just a matter of noticing why one style of bow appeals to you more than the others, why you wouldn't be caught dead using a mechanical release, how you prefer the trails of field archery over a line of FITA targets, or for some inexplicable reason why you thrive on the shoulder-to-shoulder, high-stakes indoor round. As your attention to your shooting form becomes more focused and refined, you will notice in more detail how *you* think and how *you* feel. There's a good reason why the ancient Zen masters chose archery as a meditation discipline. You don't have to be a Buddhist to benefit from the spiritual effects of archery. Moreover, you don't have to practice archery for spiritual reasons to achieve many of the skills and insights that spiritual seekers of all traditions pursue.

The Power of Attention

Whether you want to excel at a sport, achieve some goal, or meditate as part of your spiritual practice, the power of placing your full attention on the present moment is huge.

What this black and white photo doesn't show you—the iridescent green moss growing on the trees, the sunlight shafting down from an intense blue sky, the sheer beauty of this target—adds to the joy I find in archery.

Sometimes the opportunity to learn about attention is given to us by life, forced on us by circumstance. Sometimes we choose an activity for the sole purpose of developing our skills. For me it's been both. Archery came into my life because my husband was an archer. It started as a recreational activity and then, as I began to compete, archery became more of a goal-oriented pastime. Now it's my livelihood. But I didn't foresee that it would become an important part of my spiritual practice and one of the best teachers I could hope for.

I don't think "it" has to be archery; it could be anything. But if you want to develop your ability to place your full attention on the present moment, you couldn't have chosen a better hobby.

Meditation requires stillness. In archery you can bring the same level of attention to a physical activity. All religions have some form of physical ritual. The act in itself could be anything, but the attention to the spirit of the act provides an island of time and space in which to place your full attention.

Meditation takes place within us. Having something physical, outside of my body, perceived as separate from me, something without which I cannot do this activity (bows and arrows and targets) gives me the opportunity to experience in increasingly subtle ways my relationship to these objects. Many religions teach that at the end of our spiritual path we will know ourselves as being "one with everything." You can get a taste of this with the object of your practice. I jokingly say, "*Hit* the spot? Hey, I *am* the spot!"

Archery is also a great opportunity to practice being nonjudgmental. My string breaks, my sight slips, I screw up the shot. Emotions rise—pride, disgust, elation, boredom. It's all there. But it's only archery, so I try to observe these emotions, forgive myself or my equipment, and practice returning to the moment, stretching the amount of time I can stay quiet between those chattering thoughts. No, it's not easy. But since *it's only archery,* it's a much easier place to practice than "real life." I find that the abilities I develop behind the bow are then truly available to me in any way I choose to use them.

Then, without warning, "it" happens. I stop trying so hard. There is no good or bad, no me and the bow, no previous bad shot or future winning score. It's all right here, right now, and it feels perfect. Some call it the zone. It really happens. And the more I practice keeping my attention in the present, the more it just seems to happen.

One of the paradoxes of archery is that it takes *all* of me, yet ultimately I have to "get out of the way." Everything I have I bring to the shot—my attention, my training, every aspect of my physical form. I am completely there. But the shot doesn't go well unless I allow it to happen on its own. I must set up with the best form I am capable of, give it my full attention, but then allow the shot to complete itself without any conscious control on my part. If I just let the bow do its job, that arrow will fly true. This "me/not me" lesson can be used in every aspect of my life, but I think it's easiest to learn with a physical teacher such as a bow.

It's quite natural to be present in the moment when we are enduring pain or when we are in the presence of beauty. Pick one for your practice. I choose the beauty of archery. The curve of my bow, the sound of the string at release, the arc of the arrow in flight, these things are spectacularly beautiful to me. When I enjoy that beauty, I am here and now with my full attention in the present moment. For that tiny interval of time in which I watch an arrow fly, thinking ceases. If I take that experience and consciously replicate it, allowing more and more time and attention before another thought kicks in, I have a tool that I can then use at will. This ability to arrest my thoughts and simply be present will make me a better listener, both to others and to my truest self. Beauty makes the practice more appealing and makes the cessation of thought feel less frightening.

Being able to find your quiet center where the bow seems to shoot itself is invaluable in the pressure cooker of high stakes competition.

Practical Skills

The parents of the kids in our local archery program get so excited as they watch what happens when their children get involved in archery. They see the focus required, the math skills being put to the test while scoring, respectful behavior and archery etiquette, the ability to relax and concentrate at the same time, goal setting, self-talk awareness, visualization, perspective, consciously developing confidence, overcoming fear, and more. Archery offers an opportunity to develop very practical skills that a person of any age can use.

Archery is an intensely personal activity. It happens only with *my* body, *my* mind, and *my* equipment. I can shoot beside you, but I really can't shoot with you. Most of us, though, participate in an archery community of some sort. There are benefits to being a part of a community, people who choose to spend time together based on something they have in common. The community of archers has a lot to offer. The idea of receiving from one who has more experience than you while also giving to one who has less is a powerful model. When you find yourself both a student and a teacher, you find yourself. You don't need to be a certified coach or adhere to only one instructor's philosophy to achieve this. It's the simple act of asking for help from someone you respect and the gift of offering your time and experiences to help someone else enjoy this sport. This can involve professional coaching or just "the buddy system," but you will find tremendous growth as an archer and as a person if you participate in the give and take of an archery community.

Acquiring Expertise

You've made it through this book. You've heard from some of the best archers and coaches on the planet. My guess is that this isn't your only source of information, expertise, or advice. How do you see this process? Do you hammer away at yourself and your equipment and strive for all you're worth to achieve your archery goals? Do you just keep moving from one improvement to another? That's fine. But staying aware of the beauty of the process will serve you well as an archer and as a person. The symbiosis of refined physical form, tuned equipment, and clear mental processes is well worth watching. You'll become your own best inspiration.

Having Fun

Ultimately there's always one reason to shoot a bow and arrow—it's fun! There are many psychological, social, physical, and metaphysical benefits to having fun. Let's just pretend that I wrote all about them and you've read every word. Let's both nod our heads knowingly, having pondered those thoughts. Good. Now let's grab our bows, call our best shooting buddies, and head for the range. I'll see you there.

For More Information

For more information, you may want to consult some of the following sources. All of the archived articles of *Archery Focus* magazine are available free with a one-year subscription to *Archery Focus OnLine Edition* (www.archeryfocus.com).

Bows and Arrows

Dudley, John. Which arrows should I use for 3-D? *Archery Focus* 2 (4).

Frangilli, Vittorio. Arrow selection. *Archery Focus* 6 (1).

Frangilli, Vittorio. To tell limbs from limbs. *Archery Focus* 6 (1).

Gerard, Mike. Recurve bow tuning tips. *Archery Focus* 2 (6).

Kronengold, David. Sighting in. *Archery Focus* 4 (2).

Kronengold, David. Setting up compound bows–the easy way. *Archery Focus* 7 (2).

Lueck, Gene. How to level your compound bow sight. *Archery Focus* 6 (4). (*available free in "Complimentary Issue" at* www.archeryfocus.com).

McKinney, Rick. What type of fletching is best? *Archery Focus* 2 (2).

Rabska, Don. Setting tiller for a recurve. *Archery Focus* 2 (1).

Wise, Larry. Tuning your draw length. *Archery Focus* 2 (4).

Wise, Larry. Using the back-tension release aid: parts 1 & 2. *Archery Focus* 3 (4-5).

Fitness

Musta, Annette M. Strength training those "archery muscles." *Archery Focus* 4 (2).

Musta, Annette M. The importance of being flexible. *Archery Focus* 4 (6).

Musta, Annette M. Theraband exercises. *Archery Focus* 6 (5).

Form

Gerard, Mike. Good shooting form and the body geometry connection. *Archery Focus* 3 (2).

Gerard, Mike. Controlling your clicker. *Archery Focus* 3 (3).

Gerard, Mike. Controlling the pace of your shot. *Archery Focus* 4 (4).

Lonsdale, Mark. Competition stress. *Archery Focus* 5 (4).

McKinney, Rick. Conscious vs. unconscious aiming. *Archery Focus* 6 (2).

Rabska, Don. Breathing for better performance. *Archery Focus* 3 (4).

Rabska, Don. Developing the magic release. *Archery Focus* 6 (2).

Ruis, Steve. Is the dead release really dead? *Archery Focus* 7 (2).

Stonebraker, Rick. Finish the shot! *Archery Focus* 1 (4).

Wilcock, Drew. Shot dynamics. *Archery Focus* 3 (3).

Just for Fun

Pelfrey, Ty. The fine art of trash talking. *Archery Focus* 5 (1).

Mental Training

Franseen, Lisa. Does positive self-talk really work? *Archery Focus* 5 (6).

Franseen, Lisa. Making it routine. *Archery Focus* 2 (6).

Franseen, Lisa. It doesn't hurt to ask about sports psychology. *Archery Focus* 4 (3).

Gerard, Mike. Target panic—another view. *Archery Focus* 6 (5).

Recommended Reading

Bassham, Larry. With Winning in Mind. This is the book on performance enhancement by Olympic champion, world champion, and Olympic coach Lanny Bassham. Highly recommended. Available at *www.lannybassham.com*.

McKinney, Rick. The Simple Art of Winning. Available from Archery Focus Magazine (1-800-671-1140) or directly from the author at *www.carbontecharrows.com*.

This is one of the very best resources for recurve bow shooters, especially if you shoot FITA freestyle. Every aspect of recurve archery is covered by the most decorated archer in American history.

Wise, Larry. Core Archery. The Master Coach and professional archer's latest book, *Core Archery*, is his long awaited missive on compound archery form. Available directly from the author at 1-800-464-9997.

Wise, Larry and Helgeland, Glenn. (1998). On Target for Tuning Your Compound Bow. Available directly from the author at 1-800-464-9997.

Wise, Larry. (1994). On Target for Tuning Your 3-D Bow. Available directly from the author at 1-800-464-9997.

Other Resources

Mastering Compound Bows (eBook, PDF format). All the technical aspects of shooting a compound bow with a release from champion archer James Park of Australia. Color photos, some showing the form of 2003 world champion and fellow Australian, Clint Freeman. Available on CDROM at *www.archery-forum.com/afstore/product.lasso?id=7*.

Rowe, Ruth. Fundamentals of Recurve Target Archery. Targeted toward beginning or returning recurve archers and coaches of such archers, this is a step by step, no nonsense approach to the right track. Every recurve archer would benefit from reviewing this material. Especially valuable for coaches. Available from Archery Focus Magazine (1-800-671-1140) or *www.qproductsarchery.com*.

Rowe, Ruth and Anderson, Allan. Simple Maintenance for Archery. Everything you need to know about the basic maintenance of recurve and compound bows as well as arrows and other archery tackle. Highly recommended. Available from Archery Focus Magazine (1-800-671-1140) or *www.qproductsarchery.com*.

Straight Talk from the Pros (Video). There is no better guide to shooting with a release aid than this video. Hear from top release shooters how the use their release but also how they got into trouble and how they got out. Gtreat footage of great shooters shooting with release aids. 68 minutes, VHS. Available from Carter Enterprises at 208-624-3467 or *www.carterenterprises.com*.

Terrain

Mundon, Tim. 2002. Shooting FITA field unmarked distances. *Archery Focus* 6 (3).

Ruis, Steve. The very last word on shooting up and down hill. *Archery Focus* 3 (5).

Weather

Pellerite, Bernie. Shooting in the wind and rain. *Archery Focus* 4 (2).

Serralheiro, Pedro. Heat disorders. *Archery Focus* 4 (4).

Serralheiro, Pedro. Stop the sun, not the fun. *Archery Focus* 4 (5).

References

American Council on Exercise. 1996-1997. *ACE personal trainer manual*, ed. Richard T. Cotton. San Diego: ACE.

American Dietetic Association. *Athletes fuel up for fitness and weight management*. www.eatright.org.

Bassham, Lanny. 1996. *With winning in mind*. Newberg, OR: BookPartners, Inc.

Clark, Nancy. 1998. Eating before competing. *The Physician and Sports Medicine* 26 (9).

Coppel, D.B. 1995. Relationship issues in sport: A marital therapy model. In *Sport psychology interventions*, ed. S.M. Murphy. Champaign, IL: Human Kinetics.

Csikszentmihalyi, M. 1975. *Beyond boredom and anxiety*. San Francisco: Jossey-Bass.

Dudek, Susan J. 1987. *Nutrition handbook for nursing practice*. Buffalo, NY: J.B. Lippincott.

Franseen, L.M. 1997. Relaxation is the target. *Archery Focus* 1 (3).

———. 1997. Visualization 1. *Archery Focus* 1 (5).

———. 1998. Visualization 2. *Archery Focus* 2 (1).

———. 1998. Don't read this article: Goal setting. *Archery Focus* 2 (2).

———. 1998. It's all routine. *Archery Focus* 2 (6).

———. 2000. Coaching and sport psychology: Making your students mentally tough. *Archery Focus* 4 (3).

———. 2001. Does positive self-talk really work? *Archery Focus* 5 (6).

Gallwey, T. 1998. *The inner game of tennis*. New York: Random House.

Gould, D. 1993. Goal setting for peak performance. In *Applied sport psychology: Personal growth to peak performance*, ed. J.M. Williams, 2nd ed., 158-169. Palo Alto, CA: Mayfield.

Hellstedt, J.C. 1995. Invisible players: A family systems model. In *Sport psychology interventions*, ed. S.M. Murphy. Champaign, IL: Human Kinetics.

Honda, S., and R.W. Newson. 1972. *Winner or loser?* Panorama City, CA: Illustrative Specialties.

Landers, D.M., and S.H. Boutcher. 1986. Arousal-performance relationships. In *Applied sport psychology: Personal growth to peak performance*, ed. J.M. Williams, 163-184. Palo Alto, CA: Mayfield.

Martens, R. 1987. *Coaches' guide to sport psychology.* Champaign, IL: Human Kinetics.

McKinney, R. 1996. *The simple art of winning.* Japan: Leo Planning.

Nideffer, R.M. 1985. *Athlete's guide to mental training.* Champaign, IL: Human Kinetics.

Weinberg, R. and Gould, D. eds. 1995. *Foundations of sport and exercise psychology.* Champaign, IL: Human Kinetics.

Index

Note: The italicized *f* and *t* following page numbers refers to figures and tables, respectively.

About the Editors

Steve Ruis has been the editor of *Archery Focus* magazine since May 1999. He is mainly a field archer but is interested in all phases of archery, especially the technical aspects. Ruis is a National Field Archery Association (NFAA) certified instructor and a National Archery Association (NAA) Level III coach. He lives and works in Grass Valley, California.

Claudia Stevenson is the publisher and managing editor of *Archery Focus* magazine. An avid archer, Stevenson is a five-time California State field archery champion and placed second in the Freestyle Limited class in the 1997 NFAA Outdoor National Championships. Stevenson is a NFAA certified instructor as well as a National Archery Association Level III coach. She lives and works in Grass Valley, California.

About the Contributors

Rick McKinney was a founding publisher of *Archery Focus* magazine and now writes "The Elite Archer" column for the magazine. Known as one of the world's greatest archery champions, McKinney won the 1977, 1983, and 1985 World Championships as well as the U.S. National Target Championships nine times, Field Championships six times, Indoor Championships three times, and Collegiate National Championships seven times. He is a two-time Olympic silver medalist, 1984 (individual) and 1988 (team), and is currently president of Carbon Tech, a manufacturer of both target and hunting arrows.

Don Rabska is an internationally renowned archery coach and a technical advisor for Easton Archery Products. He is the primary author of the *Easton Tuning Guide*, the most widely distributed treatise on arrow tuning.

Annette M. Musta, a certified personal trainer with 25 years of shooting experience, has written the "Archery Fitness" column for *Archery Focus* magazine since 1998. She is the founder and executive director of the Pass the Torch Foundation, which matches school-age children with athletes training for international competition.

Lisa Franseen, PhD, wrote the "Mental Skills" column for *Archery Focus* magazine from its inception to 2002. A clinical and sport psychologist, Dr. Franseen began working with archers in 1994. Since then, she has continued to help archers of all levels—including elite archers at USAT training camps, international competitions, and the Olympic Games—improve their performance through mental skills training. Dr. Franseen also teaches sport psychology for the NAA Level III and IV Archery Coaching certification courses.

Ty Pelfrey is a two-time U.S. national barebow champion. He has written numerous articles on shooting barebow for *Archery Focus* magazine and is currently a member of their advisory staff.

Larry Wise is a renowned archery coach and author of five books on archery. He has achieved a number one ranking in the world three times in the men's unlimited compound bow division, won the 1986 World Professional Archery Championship, and has been part of five World Championship teams. He still competes professionally and is a tournament staff coordinator and design consultant for Indian Industries/XI Bows. Wise has written numerous technical and bow hunting articles for *Archery Focus* as well as other magazines.

M.J. Rogers is the director of archery programs at the ARCO Olympic Training Center in Chula Vista, California. A Level IV international coach in the National Archery Association, he was the lead coach for the U.S. team competing in the 2000 FITA World Field Championships in Italy. He is also active in the National Field Archery Association, where he judges major competitions.